From Tortilla Chips
To Computer Chips

Fernando Sandoval

From Tortilla Chips to Computer Chips

Cover design: Michel Bohbot, Fernando Sandoval

ISBN 978-1-7021-6537-2
tortillachips2019@gmail.com

Printed in the United States of America

-

DEDICATION

I want to thank my younger sister Gracie who has always been by my side and has always kept it real. Unconditional Love Sis. I want to thank my cousin Liz, the Tyler Island Road hottie, who encouraged me to write our story. When I was in the Teatro I was known as "Smiling Faces." Some things don't change. I was known as Benjamin Dejo #2 at a time when I couldn't be number 1.

ACKNOWLEDGMENTS

I want to thank my OG friends, you know who you are, who are testament that I was young once and shared the streets of Pittsburg with you. I want to thank my friend Ed Borjon who I have still not beat at ping pong for his warmth as I returned to the Burg. Laura I could not have done it without you cheering me every step of the way. I want to acknowledge my inspiring friend, Enrique Palacios, a remarkable humanitarian from Peru who coined my journey; "From Tortilla Chips to Computer Chips." I am indebted to those educators from my start in Primary School in Pittsburg. Those who believed in me and those who challenged me. Mrs. Betty Brown who encouraged to speak out on stage. Mrs Manley who at Pittsburg Senior High always took the time to listen to me and provide guidance. Mr. Wilgenbush who put me in the front row because I had no glasses. Balu, who inspired me to be proud of my identity and what I could become.

To Mr. Arenivar

You continue to show your tenacity as a member of the school board.

I hope you enjoy Reading this as much as I enjoyed writing it. This is only one Journey from the streets of Pittsburg

3/11/20

Fernando

Si Se puede

CONTENTS

FORWARD

I was born in 1955 the same year the Brooklyn Dodgers won the pennant (I am a San Francisco Giants fan) and would face the mighty Yankees in the World Series. I was born in Sacramento, California with the box being checked as Mexican. It is said that race is an accident of birth and circumstances can dictate the path and choices you make in life. So that is where the confusion about who I was and what I could become started, for everyone else. I am an American, however I have a treasured Mexican ethnic heritage, I am a Vietnam Veteran, and began my education in the streets, but learned compassion and respect from my Mom and Dad. My dad died in an accident when I was 9. We had no money, my mother spoke no English, we had no car, I had 3 sisters, and we lived in the poorest part of town living next to burnt out houses in what was called shot-gun houses because you could see right through them from the front to the back. I read once that if you are born into a poor family, do not know the language, have a single parent, then the odds are that you will remain poor, you most likely be on welfare, enter a cycle of poverty, engage in crime. It's a good thing I did not know that information as I was growing up. No one gave the Dodgers a chance in 1955 and I had what seemed that same chance.

Life can be a revelation, with over 60 years in the shadows of discrimination, there will always be those who remain ignorant and will not accept my equality. When I was young child growing up, I basked in the warmth of my Mom and many aunts and uncles that looked after me and my sisters as we grew up. I did not meet my real father until I was in my late 40s. I always seemed to be on the edge of understanding my identity and my place as the events of the country continued to shape my understanding. The Vietnam War, Bobby Kennedy, Martin Luther King, Cesar Chavez, the drug culture, the music of Woodstock, and racism all were backdrops to my formative years. My sisters godfather was a member of the Hells Angels. I had friends in the Black Panther party and the farmworkers movement. As the country was awash in antiwar demonstrations, I embraced the Chicano movement. I made my choices, embraced my family and the friendships in our neighborhoods, and I used the power of reading to learn about the world that I was not a part of. I read through the night, a sci-fi guy reading Jules Verne in a young Chicanos body, followed the space program, and connected with the music of my culture as it permeated my soul. I felt and saw what racism did to my friends and I protested the Vietnam War as I saw what happened to the families who sons had a lifetime full of promise and came back in a box with the American Flag.

Reading the Rachel Carson book Silent Spring (1) brought back memories of rolled up pants and sleeves and remembering my eyes swelling full of pesticides and DDT when I worked in the fields in the Central Coast and San Joaquin Valley. Prejudice and racism seemed like a shadow always lurking to hurt so many, but I saw it for what it was and I for one did not let it be at my center. It was the night to our sunlight. As many today do their DNA tests it should be realized that we are all part of each other. Eventually, I would make my way out of the fields and into the world among the best and rise above the shadows of ignorance.

I am writing this book as legacy for my only daughter to understand the roads I've traveled and for others, who may find it interesting that a poor boy can do more than he can even dream. I succeeded because of a great Mother, a loving family, finding my strength through our hardships and inspired by so many who had less than me and those who showed the way so that I could do more than I could believe. I was fiercely arrogant when I was young, defiant to a fault, but with time I used the lessons my mother and family taught me as I continued to grow as a young man. My mother, a single parent most of my young life, loved me with all her heart and always had less than she deserved, and as a young child would feed me tortilla chips and salsa to slow down my hunger. Then beans would follow in a warmly rolled up tortilla before sending me out the door to face the world. Starting from my small-town roots, daily struggles and amid the racial backdrop and drugs, I kept moving forward awash in the sixties and seventies a time of change and chaos. Living in the U.S as a Latino can both be a blessing and a struggle, but our country continues to evolve with its people who are the heart of its character. I will not outlive the racism and social injustice that affects so many, but I will continue to work with so many to educate those who do not understand for positive change and will embrace the warmth of our culture and opportunities we have and learn from so many.

Yes, I am a proud American, but more than that, I am a Chicano.

INTRODUCTION

I am a 2nd generation American and I began my life in the Cannery town of Isleton within 2 days of my birth, with a population of approximately 800, located on the Sacramento River. We lived next to the town in the cannery labor camp (El Campo) in two room shacks, among the other Latinos working 7 days a week supporting the powerful agriculture business packing perishable, just picked asparagus, tomatoes, cucumbers, and corn. It was all about the work, when there was work, the struggle when there wasn't. We were poor but we were not in poverty, at least not to us, and as kids we played not knowing when our parents would come home at times. But when they did, they filled our tiny homes with laughter and quenched their thirst, and as children we would stay awake as we listened to the late-night music that filled the air in our camp and listen to the words and language of our grandparents. For me there were no bedtime stories and no books to read.

In the summer after I turned 5, we moved out of the camp and started a new life. The first school I attended was a mystery to me and I was a mystery to my teachers. Because I did not know English, and my teachers did not know my language, I spent the year in the corner so as not to disturb the class. When my mother asked me what I learned I answered; "Nada Mama". Nothing, well my mother could not understand it and asked me why and I answered "Porque los maestros no saben Espanol." Because the teachers did not know Spanish and help did not come my way. During those early years it was implied at school to not speak our native language in school and, when we did, some teachers would squeeze our ears until they turned red and move us to the corner of the room, to be by ourselves. They would call it disruptive and, in many cases send us home for being undisciplined. After the school year I found a way learn English the summer before first grade. My Mom and dad were hard workers, but after my dad died when I was 9 my Mom struggled, still working in the canneries outside of town, trying to feed us and keep going and eventually we were kicked out of our house because we could not afford to live in one of the poorest neighborhoods in town. The start of my life was by no ways unique to the Latino families I knew and to the Black families that I became friends with, even as we routinely fought in the streets because of cultural racism. Early on I could quickly do the math and had an idea about some of my close friends and that they would end up on drugs, in jail, or in a box or how us Latinos said, "En La Caja." I was right more than I cared to be.

Growing up I continued to work in the fields to help my Mom, mowing lawns with a push mower and became a newspaper boy with the routes nobody would take. I made friends with kids who had less than me and who would feel the daily pain of an abusive childhood. We did not talk about education in my house growing up, as the primary focus was to not to get suspended from school or worse. The Los Medanos Community College, which would be built in the empty fields of the abandoned Army base in Pittsburg's Camp Stoneman, was still a dream. Like so many of the kids in my neighborhood that came from poor families I did not go to college when I turned of age. However, some of the friends that lived uptown did go and instead of working and using their backs for labor they attended Diablo Valley Community College to give themselves a chance. Being poor was no excuse for not achieving and I saw that as my older cousins succeeded.. My smart friends went to College and I went to Vietnam.

Life can sometimes be a paradox and while my friends were driving back over the hill on the two lane road on Highway 4 back home I would be half a world away and gaze out over the vast Indian Ocean at night supporting flight Operations on the U.S.S. Enterprise, (2) an Aircraft carrier with 5,000 men at sea. I have been to Africa, Tasmania, the Philippines, Singapore, Hong Kong and Thailand because of the time I was in the service. I have worked underground in the desert of Nevada supporting Nuclear blast testing, I have been involved in Finance in cities and countries such as Los Angeles, Chicago, Canada, London, Hong Kong, and Switzerland. We were too poor growing up to have a car and a bank account but eventually I would work with International Banks trying to stop the flow of money to corrupt dictators and drug cartels. I would serve on the mightiest ship in the world and would walk on the cobblestone streets of Switzerland. I would achieve more than I could ever dream.

CHICAGO-BALANCE SHEET MGT CONFERENCE

In 2010 I was invited to attend the yearly Balance Sheet Management (BSM) 5-day conference with the first day's presentations being held at Chicago's Mid America Club located in the AON skyscraper overlooking Lake Michigan. Early that morning I looked out over the windows on the 81th floor across the shores of Lake Michigan and the city of Chicago. I intently watched the window washers working on the outside of the other skyscrapers below standing on scaffolding in the blowing wind with just a couple of cables for safety doing their job. It was a sunny day and while it seemed calm on the streets I could see the scaffolding swaying in the wind. I felt a little uneasy thinking that one of those guys could slip and fall to the streets of Chicago far below, over 80 stories. The AON tower itself was 83 stories tall with 5 more stories below ground and its design and construction was similar to the Twin Trade Tower buildings in New York City. Later as I stood behind the podium I thought of my fears and the intersections of my life as I was introduced by the Chief Financial Officer of Quantitative Risk Management (QRM) (4), the sponsor of the conference, as an expert speaker on managing business and technology. A long way from the dirt of Isleton and the streets of Pittsburg.

The "Financial Crisis of 2008" (3), which almost brought the World to its knees was still fresh in the minds of everyone associated with banking and I was asked by QRM, one of the leading analytics consulting and research firms in the world for banking, to present MY views on a paper I wrote; "Creating A Center of Excellence" model as part of the Asset Liability Management (ALM) function (5). The audience was the collection of experts who were the PhDs in their fields for doing Analytical Modeling and Forecasting and to plan and make recommendations to prevent another Financial meltdown. They were looked upon as the guardians at the gates of high finance. I was in front of all these suit and ties, having their attention, the kid from the dirt camp of Isleton, the most un-educated of ALL of them, and yet there I stood.

Chicago Financial District- AON Tower with two antennae

I had walked about 5 blocks from my hotel room that early brisk morning and felt the damp air on my face as I approached the AON skyscraper among many in Chicago. After showing my credentials I was let into the building and entered the elevator. I pushed the silver button and as I started to go up I could clearly see, through the elevator glass, the other skyscrapers slowly passing and the calm blue waters of Lake Michigan as I went up. Up I went and about the 45th floor I felt a strange sensation, one that I had felt a long time before, as my ears popped. I reached the 80th floor. After the elevator doors opened I stepped out into this amazing room and walked up to the 81st floor to the Mid America Club. It was more than I could have ever imagined as a young child. There were about 20 chandeliers above the tables in the conference room as this was a private club that only the wealthiest belonged. I walked toward the back of room and gazed upon the workers, dressed in their black pants and white pressed shirts, focused on their jobs as they were preparing the rooms, with the white linen cloth for the tables, fresh fruit, coffee and all the trimmings.

I was about 4 hours early but that's the way I always liked it, be there before they expect you. It allowed me to take it all in. As I peered through the beautiful tall and wide windows overlooking the Chicago river I walked to the front of the room and saw my host, Henry Norwood, and he looked up and shot me a smile and we engaged in casual early morning chatter. I was dressed in a very conservative, but sharp looking, black suit. I walked over to the podium where I would be standing and stood behind it and peered across the room to get a feel for it. Henry, the host of the conference, yelled out to me "You ready?" "Let's hope, I yelled back and we both laughed." Henry himself had one of the sharpest minds in the world and as a co-founder of QRM, he helped build the strategic business consulting practice that most of the Tier 1 Financial firms and experts of the world relied upon. He helped his company grow into one the strongest in the world advising Banks and Financial Firms, many with over $100B in Assets and Liabilities, to understand the different facets of risk, profitability, and economic shocks. Many of these firms would shake the fortune of the wealthy and in some cases their countries if they failed.

The morning part of the conference went smoothly with over 350 attendees filling the room as Henry gave the keynote presentation and small breaks were given for breakfast and coffee. The morning presentation and keynote was about the changing financial world and the challenges that the banks around the world were still facing due to the financial crisis that was still being felt. The key was for them was to be able to understand how to model the possibilities of future shocks to banking due to uncertain behaviors, runs on credit systems, mortgage foreclosures, and political events. The unanticipated loss of wealth on assets, Net Interest Income, demands on Liquidity and run on credit not only affected banks but also the stock market, retirement pension funds, business, and especially the poor. The poor were always the most affected and the least helped. The Bank I was representing, HSBC, was international with locations at over 80 countries with US Assets and Liabilities over $200 Billion and over $3 Trillion Worldwide. I was the technical Global Relationship Manager for the HSBC in the US, Canada, England, Middle East, and other countries.

I was sitting with my colleagues from HSBC bank in one of those round tables enjoying the morning presentation. My colleagues were from HSBC banks located in Buffalo, Chicago, New York City, and Canada. My colleague from Chicago says to me; "I hope you don't screw your presentation up or all of our contracts will go up and we don't have the budget for that!!". We laughed and I told him; "Hey if you want to go up on stage go ahead, I will cheer you on !" I still could not believe that all these people would be listening to my presentation. I had included technical charts, business process and sample data analysis. After lunch there was a presentation, provided by the King of QRM Marketing, who I will call Thor. He dressed the part a bit and had a HUGE OVERSIZED hammer with him and got everyone's attention as he threw that hammer across the room as part of stunt and made a lot of noise to get the room's energy back up. He talked about the innovations his company created to help shape analytics, traveled over 450,000 miles during the year to consult to companies, and was a noted key contributor in over 25 conferences and provided insights on what the markets were doing, and what world banking institutions were and should be doing to forestall another crisis.

Then I was next. Amazing.

I was introduced by the Conference Chair and prepared myself to talk to people in attendance, and to those not in the room as my presentation was being multicast via private video feed to those who could not be in the conference room due to capacity. As I walked up behind the podium I was humbled and recognized what a huge honor to even be in this room. I thought for just a moment that nothing could happen until I spoke. I gazed across the room as the low murmurs became silent and I could see all eyes and ears upon me. I could feel the tension in the room waiting for me to speak, and for them to decide in the first 10 seconds to see if I belonged.

And right before I spoke, I quietly thanked my Mom

I was confident, but before I started speaking and just for a moment, I felt a little uneasy, like I was on a ledge, and behind that podium I remembered another time feeling that uneasy.

25,000 FEET

As the plane descended below the clouds I could feel my body vibrating and shaking side to side and up and down while inside this navy plane leveling at 25,000 feet high above the South China Sea as we looked for my ship, an aircraft carrier called the U.S.S Enterprise. The captain had told us that once he spotted the ship to be ready because he was going to go into a dive before leveling off and trying to land onboard. Some of the old guys on the plane told stories of planes going overboard when they tried to land and missed and went into the ocean below. I felt there was no way this old plane could withstand the shaking as it went down toward the ocean and the ship below. I heard the Enterprise was the biggest ship in the fleet, over 3 football fields in length, with over 5,000 men, including a special Marine detachment. I was excited about getting the chance to see it, but it was now pitch black after hours of flying and I looked out of our window with only the stars above us. I thought about landing in the darkness with the abyss of the ocean below us as I felt uneasy and afraid.

I had joined the US Navy when I was 17 as the Vietnam War was raging. I was against the war growing up like so many people I knew and respected, but I had no idea for the longest time what it was all about and received no answers from those who went. When the Washington Post and New York Times released the Pentagon Papers (6) in 1971, by whistleblower Daniel Ellsberg, it shocked the country. It showed that the President and the government not only lied to the public but also to Congress for the reasons we were in the war and that they knew that we would not win, but kept sending our youngest, waiting to be drafted as their Moms cried not knowing if their sons would come home. I remember walking out of school and demonstrating against the war with my friends yelling out "HELL NO WE WON'T GO !!" Well you just never know, because I did Go.

Even though I was very bright, I started doing badly at school in my early teens and I started making bad choices. My high school was straining due to the racial discord that was fragmenting my school, I had been a Brown Beret as part of the Chicano movement, was part of the Cesar Chavez led Boycotts, and worked to get bilingual education started in the Pittsburg School System. I had family in Los Angeles and was not shocked when in 1968 15,000 Mexican Americans walked out of high schools in East Los Angeles because the education system did not provide the right level of education and was discriminatory in how they educated Latinos, including having outdated books and in some cases no books. Some of schools even chained the doors so that students would not be allowed to walk out and demonstrate. A few years after that in the South West of Chicago walkouts occurred as well showing the widespread discrimination of the day. I helped lead walkouts at our high school as well as we began to protest the Vietnam War. I had worked in the orchards of the nearby towns of Oakley and Brentwood and I could see that most of the fields were filled with migrant workers and their young children trying to survive under the hot 100-degree sun day after day after day. I tried all summer before my senior year to find a good paying job by walking the streets of my town and going to every business. I guess my long hair, brown skin, poor clothes did not help me as I received no offer of work. My grades were not good enough for scholarship and without money for tuition, books or transportation it looked like maybe I would end up working at a cannery in Antioch, or the Steel Mill in Pittsburg or worse if I followed the path of some of my friends. I finished all my high school requirements early in my senior year, but I faced a road to nowhere with some of my friends returning from juvenile hall, prison, or preparing to go there. Some had a long time before become drug users, gang members, or local thugs.

By luck and circumstance, I went with my good friend, Jerry Rios, to the local recruiter's office because he was joining the US Navy and he told me to join with him. Jerry had become a good friend of mine as his father had died a few years before and we drove the 3 hours to Lake Tahoe and climbed to the top of Vernal Falls one summer. He would look up at the clouds and start describing them; Cumulo Nimbus, Stratus, Cirrus and all the rest. Then he would describe all the air currents and how the clouds rode on top of them and said one day he wanted to be a weatherman. He wanted to be the brown Pete Giddings, a multiple Emmy award winning meteorologist who worked for KGO-TV in San Francisco. The recruiter's office was downtown across the street from the New Mecca Mexican restaurant. The New Mecca was located close to the river and it seemed that if you were from the Burg that's where you went, sooner or later. When race riots broke out at our high school I would go to the New Mecca with my good friend Alex Maldonado and sit on the stools next to the counter and hang until we thought the worse was over. The owner of the New Mecca, a great man named Guillermo Muniz, would feed us and encourage us to stay till we were comfortable to go back home. While at the recruiter's office I looked at the glossy materials they had showing Navy Ships, Submarines, pictures of young men in uniform, and so much more and I asked what I could do If I signed up. He encouraged me to take a test to see if I could measure up and find out. My friend Jerry was busy on the other side of the room filling out his papers, so as I thought about not having a job after high school and my Mom needing help I decided to take their test.

I sat quietly at the end of the office behind a partitioned desk and wondered if I could do it. It took approximately 45 minutes for me to answer questions on different subjects including math, science, biology, some electronics and some other subjects and I handed my paper to the recruiter. He quickly scanned my answers, brought his answer sheet out, and then looked up at me and let me know the results. I had scored 121 points out of a possible score of 126. My friend Jerry who had been waiting heard the results and said; "Well you might have scored high, but no matter what you do, I'll always be taller than you compa!" We both laughed and that put me at ease somewhat. The recruiter was definitely surprised at my score then he took out some new materials from his desk and indicated that if my grades in school were as good as I scored and I had not got into trouble I could be part of the Advanced Electronics track and be trained on the Nuclear Power Program or their new Data Systems Computer Systems Program. I was skeptical at first, but as I left the office I thought about it, shared the results with my friends and discussed it with my Mom. At first my Mom did not want me to go but my future was calling and soon she realized that I wanted to take that chance.

Some of my teachers doubted my score and my abilities. They advised me to work as a laborer as they did not think I could accomplish greater things in life. But there were a few that believed in me and asked me what I wanted from my own future and challenged me to keep my bar high. I remembered that one of my teachers had once told me that I was smart enough to go to the University of California at Berkeley. But that dream was just not realistic because we had no car, no money, my grades had slipped the last year and I had no understanding about how to go about it. Even trying to go to the nearby community college at DVC did not seem possible for me. My oldest sister Irene had left home when she was 18 and that was a big loss for me. She was the one who cared for me when I was young, dressed me, encouraged me to read and would stay up late up at night as I did my science papers. She was all about structure as was no-nonsense, but she would make me laugh so hard my stomach would hurt. She had two children and lived to far away for me and passed away way too soon. My older sister Erma had a child at 16, and my younger sister Grace was still working in the tomato fields for clothes. She would be working late at night and at times as she was pulling in those tomatoes the rats would jump on her and she would scream but keep on working because we needed the money. I knew we were struggling, and our family needed the money, so I had made my choice. My Mom prayed and finally signed for me as I was too young to do legally sign a contract.

Even though I had opportunity to try the programs the recruiter talked about, I wanted to be part of the Underwater Demolition Team (UDT) program. I had seen what these guys did on television. I was an excellent swimmer, had excellent stamina due to being on the cross-country team when I was younger, and wanted to be part of a special group. The UDT program in the future evolved into the SEAL teams used for special purpose assignments and rescues. One of these Seal Teams eventually flew into Pakistan after midnight and located and killed Osama Bin Laden in 2011. Bin Laden was responsible for the attacks against the US ten years earlier. My recruiter and I discussed me waiting to join the UDT Seals but because of my scores and my profile he insisted I apply for the Advanced Electronics field, maybe working on their Nuclear program. I was only 17 years old, but he had confidence that I could learn to do things that only kids who graduated from college did, and that was an awakening for me. I would need further tooting and would have to excel to be able to be accepted. I was still in high school and had to convince the dean of boys about my choice and needed his help because my class had not yet graduated. I had already completed all my requirements and was anxious to start a new life. I had been seeing this cute young Latina from Antioch, she herself was 17 years old, and she was expecting me to be her escort at a dance as she was awarded the honor of being the queen of the event. She was thin, had beautiful brown flowing hair and deep brown eyes, and was very smart, smarter than me I thought. She was a friend of the family and my Mom was excited that I was interested in a local girl, well if you think Antioch is local because it is 5 miles away. Well that was not going to happen, and I let her know the week before the event that I was going into the military and could not be her guy. She was cool about it, but I knew she was upset and who wouldn't be, and really that was the end of the romance that never got started. She would write to me during the 12 weeks of my boot camp but after I graduated I never spoke to her again. She became a ghost of my past.

I really did not have any idea what being in the service was going to be like and what I would face. I was taken to the city of Oakland by a family friend to invoke my oath to the service. In the room where I was being inducted with about 50 other young men, I noticed a picture of Richard Nixon, the President of the United States. I was not sure if that was a good sign or not. After being inducted I was asked to go another room for more testing, and when it was time I was processed and prepared to go to boot camp. I was sent to San Diego, on my first plane ride, where I would attend boot camp at the Naval Training Center next to the Marines. I went with my good friend, Jerry Rios, as part of the buddy program, but after 2 days of being indoctrinated I was shocked as I never saw him again until 3 years later. He had been in another seamanship program and they used that to exempt him from boot camp. When I saw him during leave in Pittsburg 3 years later, after he returned from Pusan, Korea he told me the story of him jumping down into the train rails as he pulled out a man who had fallen in. He just took it in stride and said to me: "Well I was the tallest guy on the platform so I was the only guy who could do it. Everybody just stood there looking down and did not do anything. I jumped down after making sure another train was not coming and I threw him over my shoulders and climbed back onto the platform." Well for me, boot camp would last 12 weeks but I still had my downtown arrogance and got into some fights as I was bullied by some about my brown skin. But I learned quickly what it was to be in the military, I learned to accept the discipline and teamwork to work with so many others who were different than me. I became a marksman after exceling with a rifle, endured the marching and survived all of it. I made friends with some Chicanos from East Los Angeles and some others who were as poor as me. I decided to give them a hand and started helping them with their nightly studies that we were required to learn. I would write my Mom once a week about what I was experiencing, and she would write me back about how much she missed me as she was afraid I would go to Vietnam. At the end of my boot camp I understood how to work with men you would rely on, follow orders willingly even as they would yell and bark at me. Trust me learning how to follow the orders of someone, yelling at the top of their voice, that I did not know did not come easy. I was awarded the Academic Award Honor by our Commander for scoring highest among our 300 recruits during our continuous testing. Not a surprise to me, but it was to many in my boot camp and also to my company commander.

I flew my Mom from Pittsburg to San Diego so that she could enjoy my graduation, along with my oldest sister who lived there, and watch 1,200 men marching and performing. She then witnessed me, I had not told her, receiving my ribbon for the Academic Award from the Commander of the Naval Training Center and gave me a huge abrazo after the commencement was over. I walked out of that gate with my Mom and my sister and I felt proud and excited for the future. We had dinner at sister's house, and my Mom talked about working in the Tuna canneries when she was young, crossing the border when she was young. I spent the week with them, enjoying the beach, and going to Ensenada to see my Uncles and cousins for a couple of days and finally said goodbye to my Mom. I was designated to become part of the Advanced Electronics program in a Data Systems computer role. That training would take all my attention, 5 days a week, approximately 1,800 hours in multiple areas of knowledge, and testing to learn how to maintain the computers that the Navy and Marines used throughout the world. There were about 25 guys in my class, and I got to know others in 3 other classes undergoing the same training, some who had started months before me and some who started after me, but I was the only Latino among them.

Once my training was complete, I spent 30 days leave with my family, listening to Mexican ballads on our record player and enjoying all the rich Mexican comida my Mom would make. I would walk the streets of my neighborhood and see my friends, many who still had not graduated and some who had started working as mechanics, auto detailers and at the steel mill. Some of my friends that were in local gangs, doing what they could do to survive, would tell me stories of what I missed while I was away. I would go with my homeboys and hang out at La Plazita, a place where a lot of bad things happened, and they would laugh at my short military haircut, but I grew with them and they wished me well. My Mom would share with me about the time when she lived in Mexico as a little girl, talk about my Abuela and Abuelo, and prepared for the moment that I had to leave, not knowing when I would return.

That day came and my Mom and I, and one of my Tias, went by bus to Travis Air Force base where I gave my hugs and said my goodbyes and my Mom quietly said to me; "que dios de bendiga." I was dressed in my Naval Uniform and my Mom was proud and sad, but knew I had to go. I was put on an airplane and flew from California over the Pacific Ocean, refueled in Guam, and landed at Clark Air Force base on the island of Luzon in the Philippines, almost 7,000 miles away from home. The base was located high in the northern mountain approximately 3 miles next to the town of Angeles and 40 miles from Manila. I was put on a bus with no windows with about 25 others and down the mountain road we went going thru old towns and villages with the horn honking to tell everyone to get our way. I saw men in fatigues everywhere as we passed by the city of Manila holding machine guns almost at every other corner. The country was on lockdown as Martial Law had just been declared by its dictator Ferdinand Marcos (16) in 1972 and it would last through 1981. I was still trying to learn how to shave, and here I was with Marines and Sailors, some young and some older who I did not know, in heat that I thought would melt the wings off butterflies. The road was narrow with a steep ledge on the mountains as we continued our journey to the Naval Base in Subic Bay (7) abutting the Bataan Peninsula where the US military base was located. When I was young my Filipino friends would tell me about the Bataan Death March in World War II. As I was an avid reader of history I would read up on it. Up to 18,000 Filipinos and over 600 Americans lost their lives during that march. There is plaque in the Pittsburg Historical Society building honoring those local Pittsburg people who were part of it with names like: Basco, Mallari, Ripalda, Tumbaga. There are many others. This may have been history for me but for them it was real life. I remembered that as I continued on my journey. However, when we arrived the ship was gone, as It had left a few days earlier. We got off the bus and were directed to the chow hall to eat lunch and await new instructions. After eating lunch it seemed like the local mosquitos had been waiting for us and they took their toll on us on any part of our skin that was not covered and finally we were picked up by jeeps and they drove us to a small airstrip to fly to the ship. The plane itself was an old BOXCAR type aircraft used in world war II as they couldn't afford to use the newer planes for us. And off we went, over the South China Sea to the Indian Ocean.

The Indian Ocean on a windless day sometimes looks like glass and as you squint your eyes and look out as far as you see, there is no hint of land, even at 25,000 feet. After flying 5 hours we were told by the captain that we were going to land in Saigon to refuel. The North Vietnamese were still attacking all over the country and the airport was a target as well. But we had no choice and we were told that once we land, we were to get out of the plane but stay close. The pilot went into a nose-dive, due to the danger of friendly fire as times were tense and he let us know. I felt helpless as we were coming in at full speed and felt the rush of being on the edge. But he put us down and once we landed on the small airstrip we got out and the airmen started refueling the plane. I noticed right away the men protecting the airport were South Vietnamese soldiers in fatigues and some were our own Marines. We got back in the plane and off we went, but after 4 more hours in the air with the only moonlight above us, as the sun had set, we had to land in Thailand and stay overnight.

That day I would feel the sharp edge of a rifle by the soldiers in Thailand and for a moment I thought that maybe I would not make it to my ship. We landed in a very small airfield next and I could make out the trees nearby next to the jungle. Most everyone got on a couple of jeeps and off they went. There was not enough room for me and one other guy and told us to wait and they would come back for us. Only they didn't and we did not have any radios. After what seemed like way too long for me, and my new shipmate, we got our duffel bags on our shoulders and decided to start walking. I felt uneasy and so did he as we had no idea where we were going. We kept slapping at these mosquitos flying all around us and as we slapped our arms sometimes our hands would be full of blood of 3 or 4 mosquitos in our palms. Our faces were dripping with sweat and so were our clothes as we kept wiping our faces trying to clear the perspiration from our eyes. We felt the heaviness of our military boots as we kept going further and further into the jungle. We felt the heat and knew it was hotter than 100 degrees with 100 percent humidity. We passed a clearing and all I could see was trees and lush vegetation and we continued to walk for maybe 2 more hours. I was beginning to doubt taking charge and walking away from where we were told to me.

But I was young. Suddenly solders from Thailand, maybe 4 or 5 of them, wearing camouflage stuck their rifles all around us and underneath our noses, barked at us, and we stopped dead in our tracks. Another one comes from behind us and starts to yell at us in a language I never heard of. I learned back in the streets of Pittsburg that when it got too hot to stay cool. I looked around and thought for a moment to be careful as my next move could be my last. I decided to play dumb. I quietly shouted out and said, "HEY HEY we're lost, we are Americans and were dropped off back there and they did not come back for us." I dropped my bag and showed my hands upside down palms up. I had no idea if any of them of understood me, and my walking mate stood frozen in fear waiting for what would happen next. The solider gets on the radio and I hear a lot of chatter in that foreign language and then turns around and breaks into a big smile and begins talking to guy next to him. Suddenly the guy next to him says in English, "Yes, we know, we have been looking for you. If you would have kept walking you would had hit a North Vietnamese patrol. "Follow us" he said, we followed them for about almost 2 hours to another clearing where we hooked up with some Marines. The Marines loaded us up on a jeep and off we went to a hidden campsite.

I walked with the soldiers to an empty barracks and laid my duffel bag on a thin sheet, which they called a bed and then I was taken to a small building made of scrap aluminum and given some chow. I was told to go back to the barracks and wait for the next day to be taken back out. One of the older guys I came with wanted to leave the camp and go out to a town a few kilometers away and asked If I wanted to go with him. I stayed put. Well the guy who asked me to go with him never came back and I never knew what happened to him. As the sun was setting I was surprised to see these very small birds circling around us. I asked one of the guys who was with me and he told me that they were actually bats feeding on the mosquitos. I had been told by others to be careful because the tropical mosquitos would go through our clothes and try to inject their small needles into us and that a lot of men got yellow fever.

The next morning as the sun was rising I awoke to the noise of a lot of soldiers outside my barracks. I saw a group of Thailand soldiers. I was surprised as I saw these short military guys in their fatigues with maybe about 80 pounds of gear. They seemed to be approximately 5-foot tall and could not have weighed over 110 pounds themselves. But what I did see was the fear in their eyes and the haggard look of men who were exhausted and helpless. There was no TV, no newspaper, and no radios. I talked to a few of them, the ones who knew some broken English and they asked me if I knew how the war was going. They asked if we knew about the Khmer Rouge and how they were destroying the country and killing anyone in their path. I was glad I would be leaving the next day and I felt their fear, as they looked into my eyes. I looked over the scarcely defended encampment and knew that fate would soon be coming their way. They told me that they would be moving out soon and would be defending their country against the Viet Cong. I would leave the next day at dawn to meet my ship and most of these men would be dead in 3 months.

THE SUITS

Being asked to speak and present a paper at the annual Balance Sheet Management conference was an honor and I was only the 2nd person that they allowed to present who was not part of their company. I stood erect and as I looked out from the podium, I could see countless banking professionals, about 90% of them men, in their freshly looking suits with their ties neatly knotted. They came from the big cities of the United States, Mexico, Canada, Europe, Hong Kong, and Australia among others. Many had attended prestigious educational institutions like Stanford, the Wharton School of Business, the London School of Economics, and Cambridge. They had their daily conference papers in front of them while they sat in circular tables facing the podium with approximately 10 per table. They all had copies of my presentation handed out to them, had written small notes throughout the pages, and were focused on what I was about to say. Above the podium behind me and to the sides of me the details were being displayed on 3 huge monitors. This was a long way from the dirt of the labor camp, the streets of my boyhood, and the war in Vietnam. The firm hosting the conference, Quantitative Risk Management (QRM), had deep consulting relationships with over 250 tier 1 institutions around the world with 41 of the top 50 banks in the USA alone representing Trillions in Assets and Liabilities. They worked with 10 of the largest mortgage originators. I took a closer look at those tables and the organizations that were represented. Some I was familiar with such as: Bank of America, Fannie Mae, HSBC Bank, Wells Fargo, Freddie Mac, Barclays, among other banks from Australia, and England. At HSBC Bank I had been designated as the technical Global Relationship manager for multiple HSBC strategic countries for the Asset Liability Management (ALM) functional groups around the world. I had developed a new sustainable business/technology model which validated the methodologies initially for the U.S Bank and then extended it to Canada as part of a global plan.

Banks have a unique position in the world to provide loans, take deposits and provide services, called portfolios and creating wealth for themselves and their high-end customers. They have regulators, in each region of the World, who oversee the rules under which they operate and through audits review how banks provide these services and ensure they follow the Bank Secrecy Act, Financial Crimes Compliance, and the Anti-Money Laundering Policies among many regulations. But there is an inherent risk to how banks provide these services and want to profit from them and there can be a bad domino effect when these banks focus on profit and greed. In the 1980s and 90s approximately 1,043 out of 3,234 savings and loan associations failed as a result of deregulation, fraud, unsound practices, and the rise of interest rates.

The Subprime Mortgage Crisis (8) caused the U.S to enter into a deep recession, with nearly 9 million jobs lost during 2008 and 2009, roughly 6% of the workforce. The global financial crisis of 2008 was the most serious since the great depression in 1929, and caused upheaval in banking, massive investment bank failures, with banks not lending to each other. The stock market dropped 7% (777) points in one day as the Congress initially rejected the Wall Street bail-out bill and the market screamed as the U.S. was in the throes of a financial meltdown. It created a liquidity crisis which created paralyzing effects on banks in which the businesses were not able to continue to use their credit lines and loans to make payroll or extend their credit lines or get new loans. This led to a failure of many businesses and the foreclosure of many homes by people who had used the artificial value of their homes for loans and now they could not repay them. Being underwater had a whole different meaning for homeowners who lost their homes. This led to a $700 Billion-dollar bailout for the banks and was shortly followed by a global recession.

I worked on my presentation for multiple weeks and had QRM review it ahead of time. I knew my presentation would only last 45 minutes, however it was a lifetime in preparing for the opportunity, to show that I was more than people thought I would be, and I wanted to affirm that I belonged with the best. When I was asked to present at the annual conference a few months earlier, I immediately said yes. I asked permission of my bank and after ensuring no sensitive information would be shared It was approved. I was going to be in the presence of individuals who worked in Finance and had spent their years in the industry working at their craft and my presentation was 2 years after the Finance Crisis of 2008. The Finance Crisis was predated by the US housing bubble in 2004. Those in the audience were being asked questions by their banks and the regulators around the world on how it could have been for-seen and maybe prevented. Some in the audience were involved in discussions with the committees in Washington and in Europe. I provided the views on the intersection between business and technology experts in providing a framework on improving the processes and ideas of governance and supporting change as part of the cycle of business.

After the presentation I was contacted by the ALM professionals at the conference from banks in South Africa, Australia and the USA and I was asked if I would be willing to come to their banks to institute the strategy and operational processes which I had talked about. I was a very surprised about the multiple offers, but I could not. I was employed by HSBC with subsidiaries in 88 countries and I was in the middle of regional projects in different counties so the timing for me was not right and I could not take this opportunity. During the conference I would take walks in Chicago alongside the river in the early evening and think about the circumstances that got me here, the future that was ahead of me and wished my Mom was with me to enjoy what I had accomplished.

The conference attendees were invited by our host to a great Brazilian steakhouse to build relationships, enjoy the food and wine, and share ideas. On another evening I had some special friends from Buffalo and Northern Spain from the conference wanting to get the feel of the city. We decided to ditch our other colleagues and walk down the streets in the south side of Chicago. We were fortunate enough to walk into a Blues Bar as these 5 musicians were setting up. Seems like just about all the people in the bar were local and we were welcomed, and they made room for us up front, when they found we were visiting. The musicians gave us a shout out and asked us to be their guests and told us we were in for a special night as they had been playing for over 45 years. They closed the doors about 2 AM, but we stayed and drank, laughed with the band, made friends with the locals until the wee hours of the morning when the darkness turned to dawn.

I was 2,000 miles away from California and as I walked alone on the Riverwalk on the cool nights with the moon and stars above me it seemed like I was a million miles away from the days of La Raza and home. I had carved out a life of success but at times it seemed like empty fulfillment as something was missing. I stayed on for another 3 days at the conference in Chicago away from my past and with the smartest banking professionals in the world. The night before the end of the conference 4 of my colleagues and I found an Irish bar. As I walked into the bar, I could see questioning eyes on me as I made my way across to a jukebox. "Irish in America" was being blared on the television and my friends told me; "Whatever you do, DO NOT CHANGE THE MUSIC." Good Advice. I may have been an expert at the conference but in this bar, that just did not seem to matter; Welcome to America. I had meaningful conversations with my friends from Spain about our families and our history. On the last day of the conference as we were wrapping up I looked out across the 81th floor, across the city of Chicago and the blue waters of Lake Michigan, and as I shook hands with many of those PhDs, a feeling came over me, that even though my path was much different than theirs, I was in that moment, one of the suits..

THE STREETS

I jumped from the bottom of pit we were digging and stood in front of my friend Juan and squinted my eyes from the sun so I could see the 8-pound pickaxe in his right hand. Juan's jeans were covered in dirt and I could see his rage as he was about to land that pickaxe into the head of the Neighborhood Youth Corp (NYC) field manager who had come to see our work. We and 2 other kids from downtown were part of the NYC program to give us work in the summer. We were 14 and 15 years old and we were asked to dig ditches in the fields of Camp Stoneman. We didn't ask why we needed to dig or how deep, we just did what we were told. All except Juan. Juan was someone I had known since I was 7 years old and he at times had a mean streak that he could not control. The NYC guy had given Juan the pickaxe because he seemed like he was the strongest of us. I told him; "Dude do not give Juan the Pickaxe." But he did not listen to me and Juan just kept cussing and complaining because he thought they gave us meaningless work. He was right of course. The NYC guy left and came back after 2 hours to see our progress and immediately started complaining because we had not dug deep enough.

As Juan was about to strike him with the pickaxe I let the NYC guy have it;" I told you not to give him the axe and if you don't want your head bashed in you better get out of here." Well he did and I got Juan to calm down and we finished our work. Juan threw down his pickaxe and said;" I better get paid or somebody is going to get hurt." Juan did not wait to get our card signed and walked home. I had run cross-country in junior high school with Juan's brother Jeff and knew the family, but Juan always seemed paranoid as we were growing up. He kept hanging around with the "cholos" in town and hurting people as he grew up. Juan got worse when he got older, got tattoos everywhere on his body, robbed a bank and was involved in a lot of other crimes and eventually ended up in San Quentin prison. I had other friends that got involved in drugs when I was growing up and that's all they knew and one of them, Eddie, was killed by the Aryan Brotherhood as part of a drug deal gone wrong. They gave him a choice, the bullet or the needle.

I remember going by one of my friend's house who shared it with his older brother downtown and as I walked up to it I heard the voices of many people I knew. I knocked on the door and as he opened it the pungent sweet smell hit my face and he laughed as he knew I was not into what they were into. It had been known that I was a homeboy, and I had lived in the East Side and the West Side of town, but I did not do what they did, and it was accepted. I said to him as I left; "Tell all your boys I will see them at the Plazita later." The Plazita was downtown with a plaque to John F Kennedy around a small patch of grass where the homeboys from the Burg would hang out and at times the cops would show up to give them the business. Well, they showed up in a couple of hours and they wore their Pendletons and Khaki pants proudly, blasting the music of El Chicano, and waved to our other friends as they cruised their low-riders in front of the Plazita on Railroad Avenue. Drugs were no big deal and it seemed a way of life and some of my friends were involved heavily into them and had connections to LA Heavies and south of the Border. Drugs were not limited to Latinos downtown and it seemed that it crossed all races and drugs were also a part of uptown as well. I remember they were easier to get than Alcohol as I was growing up. But the big impact is when the guys coming back from Vietnam had turned into heroin addicts. Then heroin started to appear on the streets more and more and families began to get impacted and pockets of communities began to transform themselves. This was a problem around the country and not just the older brothers of my friends. Chicanos were fighting for empowerment and equity while at the same time dying in Vietnam and dying after returning home. No one really knows how many Latinos died and their percentages in Vietnam, but if you lived in our neighborhoods you saw the ones who went and the ones that did not walk back to their houses. I talked to a lot of my black friends downtown and I knew that blacks represented a lot of the guys who did not make it back as well.

Because of college deferments many Americans who were not poor did not go. The draft was sometime always on our minds and we talked about it all the time. If you had a low number you knew you were going to Nam. If your number was high and did not get drafted and you stayed away from drugs you had a chance to make it out of the streets. But we had smart guys on the street, and they had dreams as well. I remember after I had my first job at Livermore Lab a good friend of mine from Pittsburg asked me a favor; "Nando, I've always dreamed of starting an export coffee business and have it all scoped out and all I need is an Expresso Machine, can you help me?" So, I saved my money and dug deep and gave him the money for the Expresso Machine to start his business, and for a time it thrived. I did not even drink coffee, but he had a dream. We would watch the boxing matches together and talk about who the best boxers were, pound for pound. He was totally into Roberto Duran and it seemed like Christmas and his birthday all wrapped into one when Duran beat Sugar Ray Leonard the first time they fought. But he could not escape the path he had walked, and he was killed as part of a bad drug deal transaction, over $20 dollars. A life for $20 dollars, I still remember him, his laughter, how he loved his kids, and how he dreamed. But it all vanished because of the choices he made. RIP my brother.

I had another friend named Marty, from Antioch, who was my same age and was in Pittsburg all the time and when I was about 16 he saw me walking down the street on Cutter Street right about twilight as the sun was setting and pulled over in his dad's car. "Hey Nando, what are you doing? I'm walking back home after hanging out at the river." I replied. He then got out of the car and flashed a gun in his hand and said;" I just got out of Juvie and I am going to go rob a gas station, you want to come with me?" "Marty you are too much. What is wrong with you dude?" He looked at me and said: "Here, check it out, I'm not joking." He tried to hand me his gun and I did not take it. "Dude you just got out and you want to take somebody's money and then maybe shoot them, well they might have a gun too cabron. What would you do with the money? You should just go back home." He looked at me and shook his head and said; "You are too much, yeah I don't want to do it by myself, and I need to get back home or my dad will kick my ass cuz I took his car without his permission." He was a good guy making stupid decisions and he was my friend. "Well, go ahead and go home, tell your sister I said hi, and come back over tomorrow and we can hang out. I want to know what happened while you were in juvie."

I had other friends who came from strong families and who made other choices; Chris whose father owned a local furniture store; Tommy whose brother owned a local bowling Alley; Juan P who became a Wrestling Champion and who tried out for the Olympics and the Pan American Games. He later became a teacher. I remember my friend Vernon running the high hurtles on the track team and laughing with him as I tried it and somehow I could not even get over one without falling down. I used to hang with my real good friend Alex, whose brother Phillip was a biker and who built them as well, and his other brother who we called "Sneaky Pete" and was a track star when he was young. His older brother would invite us every now and then to his apartment, share his stories, and ask us what we thought our future was. Alex's older sister Vicky always knew who she was and brimmed with confidence. She was smart, funny, attractive and life was in front of her. When I was young she was a beautician and she would cut my hair once in a while when I went over to the house. Alex's family was from New Mexico and his dad was always teasing me because I liked the Oakland Raiders football team. No matter as I enjoyed his humor and he used to make some mean chicharrones on the BBQ. I remember him looking at me with those big eyes and saying to me; "Food tastes better when someone else pays for it, right." Great family and good people. There were other influences in my young life and I just had to stay away from the trouble that would suck me into the quicksand and sometimes even then the streets would teach me lessons.

I had been running up from the Vogue Lane Bowling Alley up on East 10th street and only the streetlights were on as it was late and suddenly I heard the screech of the tires on the street. I stopped to catch my breath and quickly looked at the big police car with its lights and had suddenly veered in front of my path. I knew what was next. The "chota" (as we called them), jumped out of his car, looked around the street, and then at me and walked slowly toward me. He had one hand on his baton and one on his gun. I was only 13 years old, but I already knew this officer, as he was young and was trying to make a name for himself. "Why are you running?, Because its late and I always run, because I am on the cross-country team, I replied." He looked at me and said; "I know these streets and your friends and your family." I did not reply. Then finally he said;" Well go on then, and make sure I do not see you outside on the streets the rest of night." That's how it was downtown and in my neighborhood at night, sometimes being careful was not enough. I ran the rest of the way home and heard the dogs barking as I ran toward my house and I closed door behind me, and then I closed the locks on the door.

One early evening as twilight was setting I was walking with my good friend Jesse Leanos on Harbor Street in front of his house which was the end of East 8th Street. Suddenly we were jumped by 3 guys who looked menacing and one of them had a knife in his hand and another one said; "Give us all the money you got in your pockets." I was about 13 and Jesse was 14 and these guys were much older than us. I then jumped to one side of Jesse and looked at his eyes and he started to focus. He closed up his stance to a defensive Judo position and said to them; "Come on!!" I did the same right next to him. We had been taught Judo and martial arts for almost 2 years by Horace Seeno. Jesse had made sure I went with him to the sessions and I was really wanted to learn as well. Those guys looked at each other and one said; "Ah man these dudes know Judo, f…k this, lets get out of here !" and they left. Jesse and I looked at each other and kept walking and we went to East 10th street and went bowling at Vogue Lanes. But we kept on the look-out for those guys, just in case.

At times the guys on the streets would be talking smack about their athletic prowess and sooner or later it was time for the City Park. Football was king, even if it rained, and especially if it rained. Gunther had tried out for the Kansas City Chiefs coming out of College but he received no respect. Undersized Joey Rico would show up with his horse. He was Joey's dog. We always see Joey and his horse walking on the West side and on Railroad Avenue as he headed to the Plazita. Joey's dog was huge and Joey was so short that he called him his horse. Buzzard would show up and want to demolish who was ever in front of him. Joey B was the athletic one of bunch, he worked for the city of Pittsburg, but when it was game time he was all business. They would give the ball to Rico cuz nobody could tackle him and I could hear; "Bro, no fair pulling in your buds when we are tackling you!!" I got the ball a couple of times and I felt the crunch of these guys as they wanted to inflect pain. I was the least athletic of the group and was a non-factor. When the game was done the guys would head over to the Plazita or over to someone's place to hang-out.

FROM SPAIN TO THE AMERICAS

Like most people I had great memories of my parents and my grandparents and I had asked my Uncle to tell me stories of my grandfather, Arturo Salaices. My grandfather was a printer by trade and distributed news on the railroads across the SouthWest and learned the trade from his family. As the story was told to me, when my grandfather was very young, about 10 years old, he used to help his tio Cano with his horses that belonged to the Calvary. His tio Cano worked for the Federales in Mexico. One his friends, was also part of the fuerzas de los federales, his name was Francisco Villa. They knew each other because Villa for a time was in Chihuahua when he was young and Tio Cano and our family was from there. Well later on during the beginning of the Mexican Revolution, Villa split with the government and one day his men came into the village looking for horses and food where my family lived, and they found my grandfather hiding under a bed. He had his men yank him out and then he recognized my grandfather, because he had red hair. He asked; "No eres el sobrino de Cano?" Once my grandfather identified himself Villa decided to leave the village with the horses and his men and did not hurt anyone, which he always seem to do in those days. After that, my great grandmother sent my grandfather to Texas away from the war. She knew that soon the government would take him and take him into the war to fight as it was done in those days.

My cousin, Marti Conger, worked over 20 years doing research on our family and published the findings on this research (www.salaices.com). The research of the Salaices (9) family dates back to Budea, in Northern Spain as part of the Basque countryside in the late 1500s. Members of the family began migrating to the Parral region of the state of Chihuahua in what was known as New Spain and eventually Mexico. My roots are derived from my Hispanic ancestors, but my cultural heritage is Latino. When people ask me about my citizenship I remind them that my family emigrated from Spain to the Americas in the 1600s and I tell them that we have been in the United States for a long time as Educators, Engineers and Medical Professionals. Then I ask them, "What about Your Family?" My family name is the surname of my Mother and my paternal aunts and uncles. The family name is not a common name in Mexico and over the years our family has also settled in California, Arizona and Texas and other states and in countries around the world.

The Latino/Spanish influence in California has been strong since the beginning as towns and cities were established. The Spanish names of San Diego, Los Angeles, Sacramento, San Francisco are the bigger cities. Fresno, Madera, San Bruno, San Bernardino, and Manteca are large cities as well and there are many others. Beginning in 1769 21 Missions were established by the Spaniards along the coast and we were taught in our schools that they administrative and spiritual centers as the Spaniards tried to convert the local people to Catholicism. But the records indicate much more as the Spanish Friars used native people's labor as slaves and many were killed. (Elias Castro,2004,Sfgate)

(https://www.sfgate.com/opinion/openforum/article/The-dark-terrible-secret-of-California-s-missions-2685666.php)

Most people think that Cinco De Mayo is Mexican Independence Day and celebrate as such. On September 16,1810 a parish priest of the village of Dolores, Miguel Hidalgo y Costilla, issued the Cry of Dolores as the beginning of the War of Independence from Spain. The independence movement caused upheaval and went through several stages, as leaders were imprisoned or executed by forces loyal to Spain. It lasted for 11 years but the countrymen pre-vailed and the independence of Mexico was achieved on September 27, 1821. Years later in 1861 the French, under Napoleon, invaded Mexico. Cinco De Mayo is observed to commemorate the Mexican Army's victory over the French Empire at the Battle of Puebla, on May 5, 1862. France occupied Mexico and initially established its forces and established Maximillian as Emperor of Mexico. After the American Civil War in 1865, the US supported Mexico and its desire for independence. The rebel Benito Juarez, who later became President of Mexico, purchased arms and munitions and had the US provide a show of force against France. Mexico restored its independence in 1867.

As my family moved into Northern Mexico in the state of Chihuahua they founded a Hacienda and named it of course, Salaices. This Hacienda was used as the family homestead and over time many others in Mexico moved in to take care of the nearby ranches and farms. My grandmother was born in Chihuahua and after she met my grandfather she gave birth to 14 children, of which 6 were stillborn. My grandfather was a printer, a trade he learned in Texas while staying with his uncle during the Mexican Revolution during 1910-1917 (24) riding the railroads as they distributed their papers to the small towns in Texas, Arizona and California. After the war they moved to the town of Mexicali a small desert town south of Calexico. My grandfather took in 4 other family children who were too poor to feed. My mother, Otilia, was born in 1925 in the small desert town of Calexico, just north of the Mexican border and approximately 120 miles East from San Diego. Calexico was a small town and incorporated in 1908. The land in and around Calexico was the first in the Imperial Valley to be irrigated and improved amid its desert location. The town was an important port of entry from Mexico to the United States as thousands of acres of the richest land was leased from the Mexican owners for the production for cotton and livestock. Cotton, Lettuce, Cantaloupe, Milo maize, Broom corn, Rye, Barley, and Rice were grown in Calexico. In 1925 the population of Calexico was approximately 4,200 with most of the populace being settlers and farmers. The temperature in and around Calexico exceeds 107 degrees in the summer as it is in the southern desert of the Imperial Valley, surrounded by the mountains with names such as Deer Peak, East Mesa, Superstition Mountain, and Sunrise Butte all within 28 miles of town.

Across the border from Calexico is the small town of Mexicali and the inhabitants of both towns would cross the border daily in order to work, eat and shop in the small stores located on the adjoining streets. The border is separated by a tall chain link fence and at the top of the fence is barbed wire designed as a deterrent to bar entry into the United States. There is a US Customs and Border Patrol facility maintained by the US to manage the crossing of the border.

Many of my mother's brothers and sisters were also born in Calexico. As my Moms family migrated back to Mexico to Mexicali as children they worked for my grandfather.

My grandfather was a tall and slender man with a mane of red hair and as he got older his hair receded and had a pronounced hairline. He was a businessman by trade and all his kids worked with him to learn the printing business. Most of my aunts and my uncles did not stay in school past the 3rd grade. My grandfather was well known in Baja California as he was the first experienced printer in the region. He was stern as well as compassionate. Once a small Mexican child of 9 years old knocked down one of my uncles who was riding his bicycle to my grandfather's place of business. My uncle chased the boy and caught him and brought him to my grandfather. My grandfather asked who his father was, and he was sent for. Once he arrived my grandfather took note of the haggard clothing both the son and the father were wearing. My grandfather asked the boy's father if he could allow the young man to be an apprentice and learn the printing business and he would pay him for his effort. The boy eventually became a good friend of my uncle, the one he had knocked down in the park.

As my grandfather became ill in the late 50s both he and my grandmother moved to the small fishing town of Ensenada as the climate was more moderate than Mexicali's. Their youngest son, Felipe, would spend his afternoons in the ocean next to Ensenada catching local fish and brought it back to be sold on the black fish market and take some home to be cooked by my grandmother. My grandfather used to take us as children to the beach, which seemed a block away, to play and watch the men throwing their nets in the water and walking across to catch their fish for the day. My grandmother was a smart, hard working woman who thrived on order and started her own business buying juice carts. My grandfather died of cancer in 1962 and most of the business was sold off to pay for his medical bills.

The Salaices family- Sitting: Tio Beto, Tio Felipe, My Mom, Tio Connie
Standing:Tia Quela, Tio Luis, Tia Lola

As the years passed my uncles went North and started working driving trucks for the canneries that were sprouting up in San Diego. Soon my mother and her 3 sisters followed and begin working in the tuna canneries in the barrios of San Diego. My Mom and her brothers and sisters would venture out and go dancing in the local halls in the San Diego area. As my uncles ventured out and found their own places to live my grandmother would border young female college students and have them sell jewelry that she purchased wholesale. When poor Indian women came down from the mountains of Mexico, who spoke their own native language, they would bless my grandmother's home asking for food and my grandmother would take them in and give them work.

The Tuna Canneries (10) of Southern California began to flourish in 1911 as demand for fresh packed Albacore Tuna drove the industry. At the height of the industry in the 1950s, the Tuna Canneries in San Diego (11) employed over 17,000 workers for the likes of Bumble Bee, Premier Packing, Chicken of the Sea. The labor force consisted predominantly of Mexicans and 1st generation Mexican Americans with workers coming daily from Tijuana or the local barrios of San Diego. Most of the workers were women who processed the tuna, stripped the tuna, packed it in trays and wore signs pinned to their backs and holes were punched for every tray they finished. My uncles worked as truck drivers or at shipyards to support these canneries.

It was demanding work standing for hours common and paid very little. Because the pay was meager, in many cases many of these workers and their families would spread out to the Imperial Valley and up north and work the fields picking cotton or grapes, and depending on the season other crops, and making sometimes $2 or $3 a day for their families as the contractors took out their fees. In those days even children as young as 3 years of age would work the fields as the Child Labor Act did not extend to farmworkers to protect their children.

My uncles heard about better paying jobs in the San Joaquin Valley in the Northern California towns that had canneries that were springing up. Some of my family crossed the border from Arizona and drove up the dirt roads and over the Techachapi mountains north of Los Angeles and settled in Monterrey. My Mom, 2 of her sisters and 2 of her brothers came through the Central Coast, drove up along the Sacramento river on the levee roads and settled in the cannery town of Isleton. My Mom's youngest brother stayed on in Ensenada, took care of my abuela, finally got married to my sweet aunt Teresa and had 3 kids. My Mom's cousin Herlindo Reyes, who we called Balo, lived nearby and was a hard worker but he was an adventurer. He used to run marathons and would challenge his kids to stay fit. Years later when he retired he would travel through-out the Baja Desert from the North to the South a distance of 1,000 kilometers with only a small backpack. He would travel at night with his only goal to find water. He would tell me the stories of what he had to do to dig a hole in the ground and sleep during the daylight hours with scorpions scampering all around him. One day he wants to walk the Appalachian Trail.

I was blessed to have come from such a large family. My Tio Beto was involved in the entertainment business and he and I would take walks in his neighborhood in Tijuana when I came to visit. When we would walk the mile to the store all the kids in the neighborhoods would come out and say "Don Beto, para aqui por favor!'. It would take us forever to go to the store. My Tio Felipe, who's real first name was Fernando, and who I was named after, was a soccer star and took care of my grandmother in Ensenada and almost went into the U.S Airforce. My Tio Luis was one of the hardest working man I ever knew and he taught his kids to be self-reliant. My Tia Chuy is just love. My Tio Connie, who they lovingly called Canuto, would drive from Isleton and visit us all the while I was growing up. My Tia Tula always has been spiritual, took care of her 4 girls, and was always ready to show her funny side. My Tia Quela lived in West Pittsburg and she always would ask me if I was hungry and make her specialty, spam and frijoles. My Tia Lola was a humble woman and I used to go her house and visit with my Tio Arturo and watch basketball as he had the TV we never had. My Tio Joe had the heartiest laugh you could ever be a part of and he loved my Tia Chelo and would always tease her. That I remembered growing up.

CAPTAIN KIRK-HERE I COME

CVN -65- My Home for 4 ½ years.

My family always seemed to be on a journey, from Northern Spain, to the Americas in the South and across the South West of the United States and up through California. I am but a link on our journeys, from World War II, to Korea and Vietnam. I was always a fan of the sci-fi Star Trek show on television and here I was about to land on the U.S.S Enterprise, once we left Thailand. This huge ship flying on the surface of the ocean and launching its F-14 Jets and electric A6 Early Warning planes would be memorialized in the movie TOP GUN with Tom Cruise. William Shatner played Captain Kirk and all those around him had ultimate respect and faith in his ability to lead and find a solution to any situation no matter how impossible. Thailand was quiet at 6 AM and we jumped as the commands of the men came barking and ordered us to follow them down the airstrip into a different plane and asked us sit in the rear to get the weight right. I could feel the sensation of the wheels on the dirt runway as it picked up speed and went into the air. It felt like it would fall apart with all the excessive vibrating with engines so loud you could not hear yourself think. We flew out and saw nothing but ocean and finally after 3 hours we came below the clouds and as I peered out my window, I saw a task force of ships, maybe 6 of them. Aircraft carriers never travel alone it seems. I could see how big the ship the USS Enterprise looked compared to the others. From where I was looking the ship looked like a postage stamp on the mighty ocean. The pilot told us to hold tight as he was going to land on it and had to go FULL POWER, just in case he missed it. I heard this big BOOM as our plane shuttered and it sounded like a sledgehammer had hit the plane as the wheels were extended. We came in full power and I felt more than uneasy or I thought I was going to throw up then I heard the screech of our plane's hook scrape against the steel metal of the flight deck and then the plane I was on came to a SUDDEN stop.

I felt like I was in a car accident and my necked got yanked and my heart felt like it was going to come thru my chest wall as we were thrown on the deck of this huge moving ship. We were in the middle of the Indian Ocean with waves crashing all about us. Inside our plane we were given these huge earmuffs and out we came onto the flight deck. The sun was out and as I came on deck it was buzzing with activity as more plane were taking off about 100 feet away from us and others were about to land. There was an urgency for us to move quickly. There was an E-5 Petty Officer who was waiting for me and for a moment I took my earmuffs off and smelled the strong odor of JP5 Jet Aircraft fuel all around me and it felt like I was swimming in it. The noise on the flight deck was overwhelming and almost blew my ears out and I quickly put my earmuffs back on. I watched the crew with different colored shirts controlling the landing and taking off of F14 and A6 jets using hand signals and holding special paddles. These jets would be attached to these huge catapults and once the colored shirts would drop down their special paddles the compressed steam that powered the catapults would launch them and go from 0-200 miles an hour in 80 feet before taking off the flight deck. The guys managing the flight deck operations were teenagers and they had to be careful not to get in the way of a landing jet, or getting swept off the deck by the blast of a plane taking off as they would surely fall to their deaths 80 feet below as they hit the ocean right below us. They would get an aircraft in the air every 30 seconds during full operations and it was certainly busy when I landed. I was taken inside the bowels of the ship through a maze of corridors and up and down ladders by my Petty Officer and he said, "Welcome to the Edge of the World." I was 19 years old.

As we walked into the tall superstructure of the ship, where up on top the radars would be rotating, other Petty officers called out our names and were told to follow them. Down the ladders and through the corridors I went, with my duffel bag on my shoulders, and I looked at the markings on the steel walls inside which I did not understand :03-115-3-5. I knew I would never find my way through this ship and I had better pay attention. I was escorted to a small room where my Chief was waiting for me and welcomed me to his team. I was told to leave my gear in the room as had someone escort me to the computer room where I would spend the majority of my time and also to the Combat Information Center (CIC). The CIC was the heart of the

Operations of the ship, where Air Operations, Surface and Air Defense, and Communications happened with its many sailors behind display consoles and others behind big glass partitions with colored markings on them. I met the other members of my team and we spent the day getting to know each other and talking about how we worked together.

The second day the seriousness of air operations showed its dark side as twilight was approaching and an F14 did not maneuver just right, with the waves crashing all around us, and it crashed short of the deck. The pilot had parachuted just before the crash and landed upside down on the ocean and was bleeding heavily as rescue team on a helicopter tried to keep him alive. Our Navy divers jumped into the Oceans water and worked hard to strap him into a wooden stokes stretcher. But the sea was blustery, and that wooden stretcher would slam against his head as they worked hard to help him. I had been in our CIC Final Approach Displays room when the crash happened. My chief had told me "Sandoval one day you will be in charge here so remember who depends on you, EVERYONE !" Eventually, he was right, I would be the lead on these display systems that supported our aircraft for air operations, joint task force command, and strike operations. The pilot did not make it. We had a funeral at sea and then I understood the enormity of being in the service and the value of responsibility and trust. There I was on this huge ship, still having a bit of my youthful arrogance, in the middle of the ocean, trained so I could be relied upon to maintain digital computers to support Command and Control operations, and I was the newest guy in my department. No one cared where I came from and any arrogance that I had would be transformed as I learned to be a team-mate with the smartest guys I ever worked at that time. We had flight operations day and night and the men who were entrusted with ensuring that all facets of that operation were carried out were still teenagers, just like me, and they knew their jobs better than anyone.

19 years old inside the computer room

I worked in the computer systems integration room as part of the Electronics Department. It was very loud room as we had multiple KG 22 generators always on, powering our computers and at times after my shift I would lie down next to these generators and hear the humming and vibration of their motors in my ears as I fell asleep. Some of the computers were these huge rectangular boxes that were turned upside up (kind of like refrigerators) with illuminating lights that you used to isolate issues that ran our computer programs. We had other smaller specialized computers, but these were the kings of real-time processing. We had tape drives that stored the operational programs and later disk drives to store information that was being created and shared with the rest of the task force. The programs sent information from the Radars, the Navigation Systems, the Crypto Communications systems to the Display consoles in the CIC. My bunk was on the 03-level right below where the Jets landed. Between the noise of the landings and the KGs in the computer room, I learned to sleep anywhere and anytime at the drop of a hat without the noise bothering me and continues to this day.

It would be my responsibility to work with men whose job it was to be able to maintain, test, and repair these massive and complex systems while at sea. I learned how to work with the mountain boys from Tennessee, the hills of Carolina, the farms of Nebraska, and the coal mines of New Mexico. Working with this diversity of young men gave me an entirely different perspective for responsibility shared accomplishment and ultimately paid dividends in the future as learned how to comfortably interact with those who had backgrounds different than me. At night at times when there were no Air Operations I would walk on the huge flight deck and around the Jets that were ready to go in the morning. I would go forward as far as I could and sit on the ledge of the deck and look out over the dark ocean and look up into the sky into the darkness with only the light from the stars coming down. Sometimes in the middle of night I would go to the chow hall and with so many others enjoy our "MidRats" meal that serve hamburgers and enjoy what we called 'BugJuice" which was really koolaid we believed. At sea we would have to maneuver through hurricanes, which are called Typhoons. During those times the waves would come crashing over the deck and when you tried to climb up ladders when the ship was being forced up it would take all your strength and you would feel like you had 200 pounds on your body going up. At times when we had smooth sailing we would see multitudes of blue flying fish along-side our ships. I would write to my mom in Spanish as best as I could master and the mail would be collected and delivered off the ship on specially designed planes, named COD (carrier onboard delivery), and return. My mom would write back and always at the at the end of the letters she would write; "mijo, siempre rezo para que arreglas esas computadores." I always pray that you fix those computers. The deep ocean of the world seemed so far away from the campo in Isleton and Sacramento river.

ISLETON- GATEWAY TO THE DELTA

My Mom moved to Isleton after leaving the canaries of San Diego with her brothers and sisters. Isleton's character and charm over the last 150 years is in its ability to quietly survive quietly amongst the clamor of progress. The town lies as part of the Delta in Northern California which consumes over 738,000 acres with 5 rivers that flow into it accounting for 50% of the snowmelt in California. The rivers included the Sacramento, San Joaquin, Calaveras, Mokelumne, and the Cosumnes and these rivers are ultimately connected to the San Francisco Bay. The town of Isleton, less than 800 people then and even now, was founded in the year 1864 on Andrus Island among the slough wetlands along the Sacramento river. Isleton was known as the "Asparagus Capital of the World," and rose up after the Chinese built the railroads. They created these levees from the river, and they were able to reclaim the rich peat soil which was ideal to support varied crops as farmers prepared the land to support the agriculture industry. Isleton, along with other small towns along the levees, thrived as a haven for canneries and labor camps. Isleton was one of the original "Japan towns" (12) on the Delta and at one time the Japanese comprised 31% of the labor force, next to the 41% white and 25% Chinese. These laborers would be hired to harvest the many fields during the season picking asparagus, tomatoes, cucumbers, pears. They would also work in the sweatshop canneries and prepare the canned crops for loading into trucks and barges for distribution. Trucks would travel along the levee road west down the Sacramento river toward the city of San Francisco almost 2 hours away. The truckers, workers on the barges, workers from the labor camps, and farmers would stop over in those small towns to spend their money, drink in the local saloons, be entertained in brothels, gamble all day and all night, and enjoy the opium dens.

Downtown Isleton- Circa 1950

At one time Isleton's' Japan-town had 12 boarding houses, 5 stores, 2 pool halls, 3 fish markets, tofu store and Japanese school, After the Japanese and Japanese Americans were rounded up during world war II to live in internment camps the Japanese did not return. My family lived in one of those camps, that we affectionately called "El Campo", working the seasons dictated by the crops that were planted nearby. At one time Isleton was home to 5 Cannery's with names like HJ Heinz, Libby, Sun Gardner among many. The first one was setup in 1919 as the Bayside Cannery right outside of Isleton by a Japanese man named Thomas Chew. He was the first to package asparagus. Situated right off the levee road the community itself is quiet and almost forlorn, and some residents learned to drive as young as 10 years of age. Its only police official routinely parked his car off duty in the middle of the street and enjoyed dinner and beers at the bar in the center of town.

Further up the river road is the town of Locke (13) which was designed and built by the Chinese immigrants who had settled on the Sacramento Delta. Locke is still a fascinating place to visit with original buildings, museums, with Al the Wops serving the best steak on the delta.

In the 1950s many of the Japanese laborers were replaced with migratory workers many who were Mexican, Mexican American and Filipinos. Many lived in shacks on the farms and some who lived in the camps. The farmworkers had high mortality rates, but the conditions which caused this hardship, including ownership, did not have the right to organize to force the owners to improve living and working conditions. Such was the camp in which my family settled and worked with the backdrop of fear of losing the wages they earned, less be homeless. But they thrived as they worked hard and shared the hardship of their young lives.

In the late 1950s Isleton still had 2 of the 5 canneries and a couple of labor camps owned by those proprietors and occupied by the laborers who migrated to find work along the river delta. The camp itself was located outside the main town with a small road off the levee acting as an embankment where the trucks would navigate to bring raw produce to the cannery. Further on the levee there was another small dirt road that straddled the outskirts of the camp.

Cannery workers next to the campo

The work was relentless for those working in the cannery. I can recall the stories my mother used to share of the women standing all day shifting and washing the tomatoes in freezing water with no breaks until lunch or quitting time. Many of these women later were afflicted by arthritis in their fingers. Most of the people in the surrounding town and cannery did not speak English with a heavy dose of Japanese and Chinese immigrants and later Filipinos and Mexican migratory workers. Many of the businesses in the surrounding town next to the camps were run by Japanese and Chinese. The kids living in Isleton needed to be bused to near-by Rio Vista 5 miles up the Levee road and across the bridge for schooling beyond elementary age.

The schools in Isleton were segregated as those were the times with Asian schools separated from whites. Early on the town of Isleton consisted of Chinese and Japanese as they worked on reclaiming the land while building the levee roads. They built the small stores, speak-easies and early schools. Racism was huge as the town was separated between the Whites, Japanese and Chinese with schools built to support the segregation. Eventually the labor force changed and migrant Mexicans and 1st generation Mexican Americans and other poor people were brought in from the towns of Lodi and Vacaville. In the early 20th century the towns along the river would incur yearly flooding and the Delta continually destroyed the towns and they had to be rebuilt. Later flood controls were introduced including the building of the Shasta Dam up the river to reduce the risk of flooding on an annual basis.

EL CAMPO

My sister Erma and I at the Campo

I snapped my head around and watched the light as it careened and cast shadows slowly across my room in my family's home. I was curious even then, as a 1year old child, as I heard the gravel being bitten by the wheels of a truck as it rambled down from the levee road and headed to the cannery to drop off raw produce. I was just a kid in a crib in a dark and empty room as I watched those lights wither by as part of an eerie quiet in the small two room migrant cabin. I would hear other cars careening on the levee road next to my window throughout the night and the early morning. When the early morning sun would sweep across the river it would light up our little house and my mom and dad would start getting ready for the workday. I remember the joys of my childhood in Isleton, laughing, running, playing and I felt safe and protected. My parents were laborers, worked from dawn to dusk, and my skin was as brown as the dirt beneath my feet. In time my feet would touch the ground halfway around the world.

The shacks in the camp were laid out in 6 rows and 6 houses deep alongside the levee road. Our first house, with 2 rooms, was the first house located next to the first road with the levee separating it from the quiet Sacramento River. There were two roads with the first road next to the cannery itself and the second road to the camp. There were approximately 30 families living in our camp, mostly migrant workers from Mexico, but also just poor 1st generation American laborers. I can still at times feel the dirt on my feet as I ran around the houses with my cousins at my heels chasing me or running from me to hide. The first time I held a baseball was in that camp and I used to throw it against the wall of a deserted burnt out house. We were always outside being loud, being scolded, and always it seemed throwing rocks as far as we could into the old pallets in the cannery or in the direction of the fields. My other cousins lived along Tyler Island road, next to Bayside about 2 miles away and as kids we would walk/run thru the fields to get from Isleton to Bayside and be careful not to fall in the canal. One day older cousin Joseph, who was two years my senior and was about 5 at the time, and I were playing, and he fell in the canal. The canal was used to help support the irrigation on the farms and the sides of the canal were slippery and there was nothing to keep you from falling in. He yelled and cried and told me to go get help. The problem was I only spoke Spanish and he was speaking English and I thought he wanted me to go away. No help came his way that day, but he somehow climbed out of the canal, and he still reminds me of the day I left him there to die. But he made it out.

With 3 of our families living in the campo, we had young 12 cousins who all seemed to live next door, and another family living in Bayside, with 3 more kids, within walking distance. There was never a dull moment growing up. Embraces by my aunts came often, running away from their chancla's during the day, we fell, and cried, and laughed with music filling the night air on those cold nights next to the river. My Mom and dad, and my uncles and aunts worked in the cannery and some of the kids worked the farms picking the produce that would be used in the cannery. My mom would make caldos, soup consisting of sliced corn, pieces of chicken, sliced carrots, celery, tomato, and zucchini, at night so that we always had something to eat in the daytime. She would also make flour tortillas that were warmed and filled with butter to keep the hunger away. We would climb up and over the levee to see the barges full of produce from all the farms on the delta take the produce down the river and we would fish along the banks of the levee road. I only spoke Spanish while I lived in the camp, which not unusual. English was not something you started learning until you went into town to go to primary school, and not everyone went. English was not taught, as much as it was absorbed.

My parents would prepare themselves for the day and take me and my older sister to my aunt's house so that she could care for us. The cannery was right next to the camp and it had aluminum wired fencing to keep us separated from it and had mountains of pallets that were used to load asparagus, cucumbers, and other hard produce. They would clean the tomatoes and other goods that would be canned and prepare them for shipment. The whistle would sound at noon and all the workers would hurry to the houses in the camp as they only had 30 minutes for lunch. The wives who did not work in the cannery or were on different shifts prepared the meals along with their young girls with fresh tortillas, frijoles, and hot roasted Chile to spice up the food. The men normally ate together on long tables and separated from the women and children who also ate together. The men would quench their thirst with hearty beer and share stories of nights passed and daily struggles until it was time for the workers to get back to the plant. Music would be blaring in the background to remind them of where they came come. When they had left my cousins and I would sneak into the cannery grounds and build forts out of the abandoned pallets that were on the warehouse grounds. Sometimes the forts were not sound and would come crashing down on us and we worked hard to get out. We were always getting hurt by jumping on those pallets getting bloodied by the sharp wood and nails sticking out of them.

I can recall that at times that only my Mom and I lived in our 2-room shack of a house by ourselves as she had sent my sisters to my grandmother who lived in Mexico. A couple times a year or so, I would be taken there, just me and my Mom riding a Greyhound bus on US Highway1 along the Pacific Ocean to go see them and the rest of my cousins and uncles. I remember peering out the window and looking at the steep drop to the bottom next to the ocean and to this day I am uncomfortable with the edge.

Sometimes my Mom would leave me there for a month or so and I would ask her; "Mommy porque' me vas a dejar aqui?" She would answer quietly;" Mijo portarse bien. Voy a regresar pronto, porque tu eres mi Rey." As I got older and remembered those days I always wondered how my Mom had the strength to do what she did, but she did to be able to help us survive. As a child all I could remember was dirt always underneath my feet, whether in Isleton or in the fishing village of Ensenada or the town of Tijuana Mexico. To this day I am more comfortable without shoes for my feet. Walking in the campo of Isleton as a young boy I clearly remember that my feet seemed cushioned as I walked due to the ground itself was actually peat soil when the levees were raised. When the dirt was watered it had a kind of sand consistency due to its rich peat soil consistency as it was derived from the river.

As kids we used to play next to a huge water tank, used for all the residents of the campo, behind my Uncles house and climb on top of it and see who could jump off. When we were on top, we felt we thought we could see all the houses in the campo, and we would stand as high as we could to try and see the trucks as they passed by on the levee road. We would at times sneak up and over the levee and throw rocks at the passing barges on the river, which of course our rocks did not come close to hitting. In the early mornings we would sit on the rivers muddy shore next to the levee and dig for worms and throw them in our cans to use them later for fishing. I watched as the older kids tried their luck at catching the fish in the river and paid attention as an older kid named Ismael showed me how to bait the fishing sticks and throw the lines in the water. We could see across the other side of the river and to the other levee which had a road that meandered through the small houses along the river. At night the older kids would collect us all and frighten us with their stories of witches on the river taking little kids. I was fortunate to grow up with my 12 cousins in that camp and enjoyed being part of the little town of Isleton and enjoyed my age of innocence.

I always full of excitement as at least once a week I left the camp with my 4year old and 5year old cousins and walked into the town, which seemed like a different world, and looked for my favorite Chinese store. As I walked in the store I saw multiple containers of teas and candies, ornate hand woven table clothes, little Chinese dolls and I would smile at the owner who was an older Chinese gentleman, who looked to be about 80 years old who we called Pops, who spoke no English, and had no hair. I would point to the delicate Chinese candy, wrapped in small paper inside his Mason jars and he would pull them out with his trembling hands. When we got into town we would walk into the world of the Tong in the West side of town. The Chinese were some the first immigrants into Isleton, along with the Japanese, and built their communities around the Tong hall. This is where the practices of the Chinese and their leaders and the people would gather to decide how to conduct their business and their lives. It would be used for meetings, festivals and schools to keep their language alive When our parents were picking up groceries it would be a dance of hand gestures, smiles and transferring of money. In the middle of the town the bars seemed to always be full of people into the night. The bars were full of people who lived in town, in the camp, and other workers who worked on nearby farms joined by people passing through the town.

A couple of miles away in the community of Bayside my other cousins lived with my Aunt and Uncle on Tyler Island road next to a farm and a tributary of the river. There were tall cornstalks as far as the eye could see next to my Aunts house and we could pick whatever we wanted as some of the corn was on her land. My uncle owned a small garage and gas station in Isleton, and it would be the first thing you would see as you walked down into the town from the levee road. I can still see the Flying Horse emblem and the smell the pungent aroma of oil and diesel that always seemed to occupy the station. My older cousins would be taught how to change tires, change oil and service customers coming into town. I can remember going to my aunt's house and she would put me work washing windows, raking the leaves and doing general clean-up and would pay me to let me understand the value of work and the value of a dollar.

Her son Joseph always was always an outdoor kid and he would chase the animals outside the fields of their house. He had a shack in the backyard filled with birds of all kinds including pigeons, doves, and a collection of chickens and rabbits. Never did like that rabbit stew he made. Once when I was about 4, he said "Fernando lets go next door to the farm and have some fresh goat milk." So off we went, walking on the road toward the access road to the farm and yup sure enough there was a goat tied up close to the road. Joseph had a tin cup that he had brought from the house and he squeezed the milk out of the goat and took a good gulp. Then he squeezed it out for me. I was curious and that fresh goat's milk looked good, but it was warm, too warm. Then it hit my stomach and then I let out a yell as I threw up. My cousin laughed so loud I thought the farmer would come out. He told me later that he knew it was bad but wanted to see my reaction. And even though we moved after I was almost 5 years old to Pittsburg about 35 miles away our families were close and continued to visit each other. I always admired Josephs confidence and the fact that he had two older sisters and did not have brothers, just like me, and somehow that always made me connect with him when I was young.

Josephs Mom, Tia Chelo, always loved taking the 75-mile trip from Isleton to San Francisco to shop and enjoy the shops of China Town, the dress shops and the restaurants the city had to offer. When our family moved to Pittsburg, she would at times pick me up as a small child when I was 7 years old and take me to San Francisco, ride on the Cable Cars, and teach me to learn to eat smoked Salmon and try to teach me about the best wines. My aunt was the bookkeeper for my uncle's gas station. She would bring a small satchel with their days earnings and spread it out on her living room table. She would ask me to separate all the coins and she would teach me how to count them. I was 4 years old and she was teaching me the fundamentals of math by learning how to add. She would ask me what the amounts were and then she would pay me for helping her. She would give me chores like washing windows and pay me for my work and I learned to save the money she gave me and told me to keep a notebook for what I had earned and understand the value of work and understand the difference of the coins I was keeping.

My cousin Joseph throughout his adult life never worked a day in an office. When we were young I remember that he showed me his collection of his shotguns that he used for hunting and how each one loaded. We would go out to the field and work on our aim and shooting at cans to see who could hit the most. His Mom always used to tell me to keep learning as much as I could and would point out the work that the men were doing at my uncle's garage. She always told me; "Mijo, don't let ANYONE change who you are." I think about her at times, I hear her laughter and her voice. Her journey on earth was interrupted and we lost her here when I was young to an unknown illness. She left me with her alma which I treasure to this day.

My Tia Chuy's house in the campo always had the warm aroma of the flour tortillas she was always making. She was my dad's sister and she ruled her house with iron, loved all of us, and was extremely independent and worked till she got tired of standing, then got back up and continued on. When I was older she would proudly show me her Teamsters' card. At times the cannery was extremely busy and at other times it was very quiet as the crops were seasonal and the families would have to move to another area to find work. My Mom a single mother with 3 kids would send me to Mexico to stay with my grandparents from time to time while she looked for work. She would put me on the Greyhound bus to the border down of San Ysidro next to the Mexico border and at times my Uncle would pick me up.

My sister Irene and Erma were sent to live with other relatives as Irene was 6 ½ years older than me and Erma 2 years older. My oldest sister Irene, even though she was a child herself, would start to take care of me as a young child in Isleton, as that was the custom our Latino culture. The dirt in Isleton always felt damp as it never seemly dried out because it was reclaimed from the river and I would run to my aunt's house shoeless in the campo all the while dodging the bees which were part of my house. My Tia Chuy was married to my Moms brother, who worked in the gas station and did not allow any foolishness. They had 3 boys of their own and 1 girl and I was continually with them and they would tease me all day long it seemed because my ears were oversized. At times my older cousin Luis would call me over to his house and I would run over there with maybe only a pair of shorts on and no shirt and we would pretend to be baseball players. We had no park, no field and no bats but we had a ball. We would throw the ball against the wall of a burned-out house, next door to my aunt's house, and would try to have it bounce back to us. At times the ball would fly into the one of the windows and we would find a way to get into that house to get our ball all the while hoping there was no one living in it. When the cannery was in full production about 30 of the campo houses were full of families and the camp was full of chatter and laughter with the aroma of tortillas constant morning, noon and night with music filling the night air. There would always be a hot pot of frijoles "en la jolla" on the kitchen stove and freshly made Chile that would spice up any meal with its heat and flavor.

My cousins in the campo: Rudy, Luis, Maria and Art

I could write an entire book about my Mom who somehow managed to keep our family together even as the love of her life, my dad Raul, died after 8 years of marriage. If there was a Mom that loved her son more than my Mom, I have not met her. She used to call me "Mi Rey", her King. I asked her about the nickname, and she said it was because I was the only boy born that day in the hospital. She loved to listen to Mariachi music and loved to cook. "Tienes hambre mijo" she would constantly ask me. Then she would quickly fix me a plate of fideo or a taco de pollo or asada. I can still remember her always asking me, after I had grown up; "otra taco mijo." She loved making me albondigas, chicken mole, and Chile relleno. All of her dishes were from scratch and I can remember the days she would her old stone mortar bowl and pestal as she ground her Chile. She especially loved to entertain and invite her brothers and sisters over with the kids and she would fix full meals of enchiladas and arroz con pollo and have our old 33 record-player on. My dad would turn off the record player at times and bring out his guitar and begin belting out Mariachi tunes late at night and I would hear all the women crying as they remembered the words and felt the pain of the songs. As I was growing up my Mom did not know English and I would trick her when the school would send me home under suspension with notes explaining why. I just had her sign the paper. If I could give her just one more hug, now that would be my dream.

When I was older my mother used to tell me stories about the racism when she was working in the Tuna canneries in San Diego. When she moved to Isleton following her brothers and sisters she left her first child, my sister Irene with my grandmother in Mexico to take care of her until she was almost 5 years old. That's how it was done in those early days. The children would be cared for by relatives when their parents looked for work far away from home. My Mom would leave during the seasonal transitions at the cannery once a year to visit with my oldest sister. After 5 years my Mom returned to Mexicali to pick up my sister and brought my older sister Erma, who was 2, and me as a baby and reunite us as a family, but all of us were strangers to Irene. It was a hardship however my mother loaded up my oldest sister and the four of returned to Isleton on one of my uncles old Buick and he accompanied us on the long trip back to Isleton which took about 18 hours in those days due to the unpaved roads and stops we had to make. After my younger sister was born, when I was 2 years old my Mom and dad continued to work in Isleton together. Eventually, 3 years later, the canneries began winding down and my dad got a job in the neighboring town of Antioch, 20 miles away from Isleton, and prepared to move us to the steel city town of Pittsburg which was called Black Diamond in its early life.

BLACK DIAMOND

Surveyed as "New York of the Pacific" in 1850s the location of the town of Black Diamond was at the mouth of where the San Joaquin and Sacramento rivers join or part of the deep waters of Suisun Bay. The town attracted fisherman who brought their families as they enjoyed the calm waters (14). Considered for military use the town was originally named Black Diamond after the discovery of coal at the foothills of Mount Diablo in Nortonville next to the town. The 6-mile two lane road of Kirker Pass alongside the small hamlet of Nortonville was the main road over the hill into the small town of Clayton. It was a steep and treacherous road with many cars careening off the edge of the road both coming back into town. The road with dangerous often with a thick fog and no lights to provide guidance over the hill with cars driving over the edge into the canyons below. Small produce vendors worked at the foot of Kirker Pass on Nortonville selling their wares to those coming into town. The discovery of coal began the transitioning of the town from a small hamlet known for its fishing, but it would continue to transform itself. Large barges would transport agricultural products grown in the San Joaquin Valley along the Sacramento river next to the town of Black Diamond and further to Martinez and San Francisco. Canneries began to sprout up to pack these perishable products. Early on fishing was the primary occupation of many of its inhabitants as they caught sturgeon, sardines and bass. An economic collapse in Sicily around 1890 created a mass migration to Pittsburg from the "Isola delle Femmine" (15). The Island is located on the Mediterranean coast in Northwestern Sicily approximately 15 km from the city of Palermo. It is estimated that half of the population participated in the migration as they took steamships to Ellis Island with some settling in New Jersey and the majority taking trains toward the city of San Francisco heading to the town of Black Diamond.

The fishermen used their lampara (lightning net boats) to catch the fish in the river and dump them onto their boats. By the turn of the century they had turned Black Diamond into an Italian Fishing village of 2,000. F.E Booth Cannery was established to support this industry on waters at the foot of downtown. The discovery of coal led to the building of the Columbia Steel manufacturing site, which later became US Steel and other manufacturing companies soon relocated due to the water access and the railroads of the Southern Pacific and the Santa Fe. It was renamed Pittsburg in approximately 1911 representing a future manufacturing vision. When sardines were found to be plentiful in Monterey, Booth built a bigger facility as they caught as much as 7,000 tons a day and began the establishment of Cannery Row further south. The salmon went elsewhere due to the dam that was built upriver. In Monterrey as the sardines were overfished those industries died out as well.

The new manufacturing companies being established in Pittsburg, included; Columbia Steel in 1911, Dow Chemical in 1916, Johns Mansville in 1926. Commercial fishing was eventually outlawed on the waters in Pittsburg in the 1950s and the smaller canneries in Pittsburg were shutdown. Eventually the fisherman of Pittsburg gave up their nets and began working at the manufacturing companies and became businessmen. The onset of World War II led to the establishment of Camp Stoneman, opened in 1942 and closed in 1954, an Army base in Pittsburg. With the industrial base growing and the military presence in Camp Stoneman downtown Pittsburg flourished with many small restaurants and stores littering the streets with over 35 bars established. Camp Stoneman served as a major staging area for soldiers who were transported to San Francisco and went on ships to fight during World War II and Korean Wars. After the wars many post military families moved to Pittsburg. Still small by city standards, the population of Pittsburg in 1950 was 12,763 and increased to 21,423 by 1970. Due to failure of businesses and loss of jobs associated with the closedown of the Army base, the move of manufacturing out of Pittsburg, and the move of residents to nearby Antioch and West Pittsburg many stores in downtown Pittsburg continued to close. Neighborhoods started to fade with many families leaving to the surrounding towns and Pittsburg began to change.

The lower part of Pittsburg, close to the river, had many stores as part of a rich downtown community but eventually due to job loss, the growth of nearby communities of Antioch and Concord, the new Sun Valley Mall, the poorer neighborhoods with outdated housing stock could not sustain business. The upper part of Pittsburg separated by the railroad tracks generally had the better housing and separate schools creating racial divisions separated by this geography. The schools in Pittsburg had athletes who would end up being All Americans in Swimming, Football and Track including NFL Football players: John Henry Johnson, Lionel Aldridge, Altie Taylor, John Henry Johnson. Pittsburg's own, Eddie Hart, was the 4x4 100 Meter Olympic Champion in 1972. In 1963 the Pittsburg Pop Warner Mallards football team was undefeated and unscored upon was scheduled to enjoy a pre-game breakfast with President John F Kennedy. However, the President was assassinated, and the team attended his funeral. Although bittersweet. the team won the National Championship. Pittsburg was not immune to the feelings of racism and social injustice with killing of Martin Luther King Jr in April of 1968 resulting in multiple riots at the High School, along with rage felt in Los Angeles, Detroit and Chicago. But we overcame it. One of the great things about the Pittsburg community is its diversity of people and a strong sense of belonging to the town. Yes, my friends were brown, black, Italian, Puerto Rican, Mexican, Filipino and as we grew up we had respect for each other and no matter where we went we were from THE BURG.

PITTSBURG-A NEW BEGINNING

The 1950s were a time of my family working in the canneries of San Diego and Isleton and driving trucks bound throughout California, Washington and Oregon. It was also a time of the Korean War, the Hydrogen Bomb program, the introduction of credit cards in the US, Presidents Dwight Eisenhower and John F Kennedy, Fidel Castro coming to power. The 50s was also when the advent of civil rights was becoming alive, Elvis, the first satellite (Russian) circling the earth, the age of computers was becoming a reality, and the decade in which I was born. The average wage was $2,900 per year. So much of the chaos and change of the 50s seemed a million miles away from the labor camp in Isleton, but the 60s was on its way.

My family moved out of Isleton in 1960 and to the town of Pittsburg about 26 miles away as the work was winding down. I was not yet 5 years old and I still could not speak English as we moved to this great big town. Isleton gave me warmth and comfort and Pittsburg would be a whole new world.

When I moved to Pittsburg some of our cousins moved in with us and we all stayed in prefabricated houses in a section of town called Columbia Park situated at the border of El Pueblo, a poor part of town consisting of approximately 95% black families. It was affectionally called The DIP through my teens with many of my friends in school living there. You only went into THE DIP if you lived there or if you wanted something to prove. The homes in Columbia Park were built by the Columbia Steel company and housed transitional families. As Camp Stoneman closed down in 1954 Columbia Park was offered for public use. Most of the families in lived in the Columbia Park project were very poor when our family moved in. I experienced first-hand what it was to be looked at as being different and I remember that at that young age I was picked on by older kids and got in a lot of trouble and fights with the neighborhood kids. Because I did not speak English and I was shy many kids wanted to find out how tough I could be. In Columbia Park I learned to protect myself, tried to pick up the English language while my parents would work during the day and evening.

We would have sometimes 2 or 3 families in each one of these houses, as there were not enough to go around. We moved to a small street called York Street in downtown Pittsburg because its proximity to the schools we would attend and also because the rent was dirt cheap. Many houses in my new neighborhood were empty because fire had consumed them. It was considered the bad part of town and separated by the local train tracks. Lots of poor people, brown, black and white were our neighbors. But for our family it was a step up from the camp in Isleton and Columbia Park. My dad was a stern disciplinarian, with the belt not far away, and a musician who played guitar and sang with local Latinos. My dad was born in San Bernardino in Southern California and later when he was 5 his family moved to Mexicali, Mexico. When he was 14, he went to his grandfather's ranch in Sinaloa, Mexico to mend fences, work horses and clear the land. He learned how to fix and drive trucks and returned to the US three years later to Salinas in 1945 and worked for the Merrill Packing Company working in Fresno. He was inducted into the Army and went to basic training at Fort Ord in Monterey as the war was heating up in Korea. After basic training he was sent to Camp Stoneman in Pittsburg by the Army , along with so many soldiers across the United States, and would trade stories with his friends and got to know Pittsburg before he was shipped off from San Francisco across the Pacific to a camp in Sasebo Japan and into Korea in 1953 as part of the 35th Infantry Regiment.

My dad on the left on the way to the Korean War

My dad was discharged in 1955 and upon his return visited his sister in the Campo in the town of Isleton where he began working, married my Mom, and moved us to Pittsburg in 1960.

My dad was not the only one in my family who served for our country. My Moms cousin, Uncle Frank, served in World War II with a tank regiment and was victorious in North Africa battling the German General Erwin Rommel, who was also known as the Desert Fox (25). Rommel had been an outstanding tactician in World War I and as a young German office defeated the French and the Italian armies fighting in the mountains of those countries. In World War II Rommel successfully defeated the French, in Belgium and the Netherlands as part of hard-hitting campaigns. He was the commander of the Afrika Corps with the 7th Panzer tank division as he defeated the allies in many battles in North Africa and gained the respect of the French and the Americans. He was later implicated in the plot to kill Hitler in 1944 and was asked to commit suicide in an agreement with the Nazi's who kept his honor alive for the German peoples.

Years later I was looking for a speaker for my Rotary club in West Palm Beach, Florida and I was asked to call Mr. Albin Irzyk who I was told was a patriot. I called upon Mr. Irzyk and he told me that he was not allowed to do public presentations, but he would be glad to receive me at his home. Turns out that he was the retired Brigadier General and served under Patton in World War II as his battalion tank commander and went across Europe after Normandy and was in the Battle of the Bulge. He was 99 years old and his memory was sharp as he talked about his childhood and how he went from a small town to college and in the Army went from horses, to tanks, to helicopters as part of the 14th Armored Calvary. His troops liberated the first concentration camp in Germany and he also served and commanded during Vietnam and withstood the Viet Cong attack on Saigon as part of the Tet Offensive. He took a liking to me and invited me to him home on multiple occasions. I remember that when I would ring his doorbell at his home and announce that I had arrived he would boom out; "FERNANDO !!!" and I would hear him shuffle with his walker to his front door. I listened quietly, taking notes, as he described his life which he has published in multiple books. One day as I was taking notes he cleared away the top of his coffee table. I was amazed, here underneath the glass of the table I saw a ton of his decorations: 2 Silver Stars, 4 Bronze Stars, 2 Purple Hearts, Distinguished Service Cross, 11 Air Medals and more. He was truly an American Hero. He was my friend and he enjoyed sharing his stories with me. He told me that before going overseas he started baseball games with the soldiers and got to know most of them. I had brought him a customized plate of chocolates for him and his wife Evelyn. She wanted to marry him when the World War II started but he did not want to burden her with uncertainty and be a war widow and he said; "When I return then maybe we will tie the knot." He told me this story. "We were given orders to cross this open bridge with our tanks and battalion to take the next town. We knew that the Germans found out we were coming and that they would blow up the bridge as we crossed. It was a suicide order, but we followed orders in those days, without question. So that early morning I gave the order and I was on the lead tank and miraculously the Germans had retreated and did not blow us up." He told me that 50 years later he went with his grandkids and family back to the town as they were dedicating a park for him. Then he finished the story. "I was in the park and this little girl took my hand and said follow me, my grandma needs to talk to you." He said he followed her on the cobblestone streets to her grandma's house, where she was waiting, and they went in the little house. Her grandma got up from her chair and then she said; "I've been wanting to tell this story for 50 years and now are here to hear it." The General was amazed as she said the following; 'The night before your troops came we invited all the officers and the SS into our home for drinks and we poured everything into them until they passed out. That evening many of our young men climbed the overpass bridge which you use to come into town. And one by one these men in the darkness cut the barbed wires from the detonators and dynamite underneath the bridge." For the men under his command who perished he wrote personal letters to their families. He said to me as I talked about his decorations; "My medals belong to the men that were under my command who did not make it." He passed away in the fall of 2018 and encouraged me to write my story.

My dad, 2nd from the right, in Korea with 35th Infantry machine gun placement team.

YORK STREET

"Mijo, bajarse del el arbol. "I could hear my mother's voice coming from inside our house on York Street pleading for me to come down from the high tree that I had climbed. It was late in the afternoon and the shadows started to creep on the front of the house. The house had these huge steps that seemingly I had to climb to get onto the porch. My mother was inside our house bathing my 3-year old little sister in a large tina, essentially a small tub, and she couldn't come outside. Our house was in the back of my friend's house on York Street and I had climbed up about 15 feet and I felt I had become stuck. I felt afraid as I looked down and knew that if I slipped just a little bit on the tree branch that I was on I would not be able to stop my fall. I climbed up that tree because I saw Tarzan do it and if he could do it, I could do it. I cried out to my friends to help me down; "Salito help me, I am stuck." But Salito was in the street in front of the house and he could not hear me. Sitting up in the tree I could see all the bees in between our house and the front house I knew my friends did not like to get stung when then went to my house.

I was already into sci-fi and as it got a little darker I pretended I was one of those astronauts I saw in the newspapers and I stayed put. My Mom yelled at me to get down one last time and I tried to get down carefully. But as I started climbing down the branches I felt the pain on my feet as I did not have shoes on when I went up. Then it happened. I slipped and down I went and felt the pain instantly as I stuck my right arm and it broke as it crushed as it slipped on the cement and was yanked underneath my back. My Mom came running out as she heard my scream and carried me inside the house, and she laid me down on the couch and ran the hot water to wet some towels and wrapped them around my arm. I was foolishly brave as I went up that tree, but those feelings did not last once I looked down and I felt uneasy as I wondered what would happen next. Eventually my dad took me to the doctor's office, and they outfitted me with a cast on my arm. I was a risk taker, even then at the age of 6, and I thought I could do anything, and I wanted to be an astronaut. I did not realize that my black framed coke-bottle glasses that I was always wearing would keep me from that dream.

Two weeks before the father of my friends that lived in the front house came to our front door and knocked loudly. I was playing with my friend Salito, and we followed my dad to the front door and stepped out onto the porch. I could see Big Mike below the stairs with his two young sons, Adrian and Tommy, right behind him. They seemed like they were about to get it from their old man. He told my dad that I had been on his roof and broke one of his windows and my dad looked at me intently. My dad was a short and stocky man who had served in Korea and he would bring down his discipline if I did the wrong things. He asked me if I broke the window and I looked down at my friends, and I knew I could not tell their dad that they did it. I told my dad that I broke it and Big Mike said that I better get the cinto (belt) and that my dad needed to pay for the window. He walked away with his two kids and as he walked through the alley my dad asked me why I broke the window. I told him that I really did not break that window, but I did not want Adrian and Tommy to get the belt from their dad, Big Mike. My good friend Salito then looked at my dad and told him that he knew I did not break it. We had been on their roof using an old wooden ladder, but Adrian was the one who actually broke it. My dad looked at me and told me to watch out and be careful who my friends were and walked back into the house. They never said thank you and I never asked and the next day they were still my friends because that's just the way it was on our street.

When I was about 7 years old my dad came home with another family in his car. Turns out they were my relatives. My tia Esperanza, my tio Alfredo, and my cousins, Carmen, Magda, Norma, Cecelia, Alfredo and their young baby Alex. They were living in squalor in the South-Central valley town of Hanford in the middle of a desert farmland. My aunt's mother sent my dad a letter outlining the poverty they were in and with winter approaching my dad drove from our town in Pittsburg and South for hours on the two-lane road to where they were and waited until they came back in from the grape-fields. He bought all the girls dresses and in the beginning his brother-in-law protested but my dad said he did not come to talk. By the time they got back to our house it was 2 o'clock in the morning and all of us kids woke up to see our new cousins and aunt and uncle. My mom took out some tortillas and beans she had made earlier in the day and fed everyone before they all went to sleep whether we could find a place for all of us. My younger cousin Cecelia, who was 4, did not know English but my sister Graciela, who was also 4, instantly bonded with her and would help her master the new language.

My dad worked in the cannery in Antioch and he quickly procured a job for my hardworking Tio. My Tia Esperanza helped with all the kids in the house because we went from 4 to 9 kids in one day. When my Mom and dad would be at work in Isleton and Antioch my Aunt would look after us until they returned from work. They would work 7 days a week during the season. It was an exciting time with my cousins in the house. We shared our beginnings in Pittsburg together. My aunt who previously worked as a seamstress, ironed clothes, worked in a bread store and in the fields, quickly made friends in the neighborhood. They would call upon her to help them prepare meals and she would take her girls to learn the value of helping others. Eventually they moved to the house next door and we continued our close family ties.

It seemed that when I first moved to Pittsburg I was out of place in this new world where English seemed like the foreign language. I do not remember my dad so much as he was always working, as was my mother. But I also had some good friends in those neighborhoods, and nobody told me they were troublemakers, what did I know. My youngest sister was 3, I was 5, my two older sisters were 7 and 11 respectively. My oldest sister took on the responsibility of watching over me and raising me as my Mom was constantly working. Eventually some of cousins, who also lived with us in the home in Columbia Park, moved a few blocks away and I would wander over to their house and watch my Uncle and my older cousins Art and David constantly work on their old cars. I would hang out with my cousin Robert who was 2 years older and stronger and smarter than I thought I could ever be. Robert had two sisters, Lilia and Yolanda who were also both very smart and would go on to college. He introduced me to baseball cards, Yogi Berra and the Yankees. He introduced me to the music of the Beatles, the Beach Boys, and Jefferson Airplane. My parents, and aunts and uncles only wanted to hear Rancheras, Cumbias and other Mexican music and all of them were San Francisco Giants fans.

I did learn English, as a boyhood friend helped me learn during the summer after I turned 6. It was either because he was a good friend or maybe I had a crush on his sister, or her on me. In those days there were no bilingual classes, it was English or nothing. I would watch cartoons and sound out the voices so that after a while my accent went away. One day my father brought home a World Book encyclopedia set, and I started reading as much as I could. Reading was like food to me as I began to understand about other countries, people, the world, science and biology. It was an awakening. During that summer I was so consumed by learning English I had forgotten to speak Spanish, such was my determination, and it nearly cost me.

It was during that summer when I was with my mother staying at my grandmother's house in Ensenada Mexico. In those days the streets were all dirt and there was a conclave of houses outside the main street which ran along the Pacific Ocean. There was only one paved road and it was located in the center of town. The town in those days was a fishing village and my grandfather used to take us kids to the beach while my uncles fished for hours. At times I would join my Mexican cousins on trips to the town to get medicine, candy and whatever else was needed. One day, on a dare on a visit to the pharmacy in town, during the early afternoon about 4:30 PM, my cousins asked me to leave the truck we were riding in. I jumped out and walked to the corner and back. Well I got lost and by the time I came back, the truck and my cousins were gone. There I was, 5 years old, in Mexico, alone, and lost.

I had forgotten Spanish, as I was learning English. I was determined to find my way back and I walked for about 2 hours down the side streets looking for my grandmother's house. I went back to the town to retrace my steps. I had been alone over 3 hours trying to find my way and the evening darkness came and the cold was starting to set in. I walked inside multiple tourist stores asking for help, but they did not know English and did not understand that I was lost. By luck I went inside a business and found some adults that spoke a little English and once they found out I was lost I joined them in their car to look for my grandmother's house. It was hard to see going down the streets as darkness had arrived and there were no streetlights to help us see our way. We almost abandoned the search, but we gave it one last try and then I saw it; the small white fence in front of my grandmother's house. I told them I was sure it was my Nana's house. As It turned out the man who was driving the car was a soccer teammate of my Uncle and he recognized the house.

I walked thru the broken gate and yelled for my Nana and she ran to the door and squeezed me tight. My Nana quickly asked "Mijo te estamos buscando, donde estabas?" I did not answer her as I knew I was in trouble. So, I quickly ran into the house into a bedroom and got a cover and pulled it over me and was happy I was home. I remember my Tios and Tias coming into the house and everyone thinking I was scared and tired and to leave me alone. My Mom finally came into the room and whispered into my ear; "Mijo, queres un taco?" "Si Mama "I answered. That taco sure did taste good, so I had two. Years later, when I was in my 30s my uncle took me to a night-club and re-introduced to the man who saved me that night.

In my youth I would follow the Giants, hated the Dodgers, and I would listen to voice of Russ Hodges on the radio. A little know bit of trivia here, Russ Hodges called the heavyweight boxing rematch between Sonny Liston and Muhammad Ali for the title on May 25, 1965. Sonny Liston was the most feared heavyweight boxer of his time. He had served time in jail and the mafia got him out of jail and as condition Frankie Carbo owned the majority of Sonny Liston's contract. Carbo was a one-time mob hit man and senior member of the Lucchese crime family. Liston was so feared that nobody wanted to get in the ring with. Henry Cooper's manager had said; "We don't even want to meet Liston walking down the same street." A young Cassius Clay had shocked the boxing world in 1964 when he won the title and then announced his name change to Muhammad Ali after the fight and became known as one of the greatest heavyweight boxers of all time. He was poet and always provided colorful quotes; "I'm the greatest fighter in the world, I float like a butterfly and sting like a bee"; "His hands can't hit what his eyes can't see." Muhammad Ali won the boxing gold medal in the Olympics in 1960 and 36 years later, in 1996, he lit the Olympic flame in Atlanta to start the games. My Mom did not like Muhammad Ali, and I remember her saying; "Esse hombre se cree mucho!" But I admired him then and to this day. But Russ Hodges was the man and I used to see old clips of him calling the Bobby Thomson home run in the 9th inning, when the Giants won the Pennant over the Dodgers in 1951 in a playoff game; "THE GIANTS WIN THE PENNANT, THE GIANTS WIN THE PENNANT, THE GIANTS WIN THE PENNANT!" As I followed the Giants on the radio, I kept the box scores and did math for batting averages, adding up the homeruns, hits and walks for the hitters and earned run averages and wins and strikeouts for the pitchers. I would update the statistics for each player once that game was over in a little black 3 ringed notebook. The next day I would replay the game quietly pretending I was Russ Hodges on the radio in the front room of our house. I knew the players intimately on the Giants; Willie Mays, Juan Marichal, Gaylord Perry, Willie McCovey, Orlando Cepeda, Jim Ray Hart, Jim Davenport, the Alou brothers. But year in and year out the San Francisco Giants would find a way to lose, going as far as the World Series in 1962 only to lose in the last at bat with Willie McCovey at bat when he got wood on the ball and hit a line drive that was caught by their shortstop, ironically to those New York Yankees. The Dodgers had the pitchers, the Giants had the hitters.

My dad took me to one Giants game in San Francisco when I was about 6 years old and he told me that when he was in the Army in Korea, Leo Durocher, Hoyt Wilhelm and some other Giants, came to their camp told them stories about the World Series and shared laughs with the soldiers in his regiment. The famous Joe DiMaggio, ironically of the Yankees, had roots in Pittsburg, as his father emigrated from Sicily to Pittsburg. The DiMaggio family were fishermen and his dad sent for his wife four years later with Joe being born in Martinez.

In Isleton it seemed like most of my friends were my cousins from my immediate family and I made friends with the kids in the campo. In Pittsburg the friends that I had started making were the ones who lived in the poorly lit neighborhoods and were as poor as my family. It seemed like all my friends who lived downtown had nicknames; Blackbird, Buzzard, Scur, Black Sambo, Chicken Head, OD, Chief, G-Jaw, Big Ivan, Flaco. My neighborhood was really a community onto itself and our house was only 6 streets away from the river. There were no parks close-by, so we played baseball and football in the streets always on the lookout for unsuspecting cars who did not see us. At times we walked down to the river where some of my friends played in the old Booth Cannery on the river's edge. They would go upstairs to the second floor and go down a makeshift slide and throw their legs out to stop before they fell through the open hole in the floor to the cement one story below. We would go to the City Park and play football with the older brothers of my friends and play till dark and through the rain.

We would go to the Boys Club and proudly display our card to get in so that we could test out our skills in basketball. As I grew up, I would go the local theater, the Vogue, and see the matinees. It was there that I was transfixed by Flash Gordon and my mind was sparked with this Science Fiction. I started reading the sci fi comic strips and then my curiosity took off. I started reading books I picked up at school and my aunt used to tell me that when I came inside after playing outdoors, if I was not reading a book I would get a headache as my mind was filled up with so many questions and ideas. My dad saw my interest and saved his hard-earned money and bought a World Book Encyclopedia. I could not put them down even as my friends asked me to play outside. I would go with them and enjoy the entire day outside, but once inside I would search for a volume of the encyclopedia set and immerse myself in it and at times read certain volumes more than 4 times over, cover to cover.

One day my dad took me to the newly built Anthony Davi library which was located across the tracks and by the freeway. After filling in the forms I received a library card. It was the best gift I could have ever receive and I made sure I knew the way to the library, about 2 miles away, and I made sure that my library card was always kept in a safe place. I would walk back and forth to the Library almost every weekend to pick out a book. The Library was a magical place. I had taught myself English and found I could read faster than anyone I knew and could remember all I gazed upon. I started reading Jules Verne, Isaac Asimov, history, mathematics, and many others. Because I had read and retained so much when I went to elementary schools, I was a good student. All the while my neighborhood was still rough by most standards as fights were not un-common. The neighborhood got poorer as many people lost their jobs and in the summer I would go stay at one of my relative's house at times. I would pick vegetables and fruits and feel the rashes of the chemicals of the fields as the chemicals penetrated my young skin.

Living downtown in Pittsburg was considered by many to be un-safe and there were lots of fights, drugs, and robberies. I can recall that as a young newspaper boy, when I would go to collect the monthly cost of the paper, sometimes the houses would be eerily quiet. In some cases, a few times they would let their dogs out so I would not come to the door. I would see first-hand what happens to those who lose hope and thrive on drugs in the dark corners of some of the houses that I delivered the paper to. I had good friends that got good jobs when they grew up. But, some of my friends ended up running gangs and some ended up in Soledad prison and San Quentin. Still others vanished as life took the life out of them, and others had their lives taken away too soon.

1965

In the summer when I was 9, I was playing with my model airplanes that I had put together and enjoying them outside my house on York Street and then the telephone rang. I ran inside and picked it up. A woman on the line asked for an adult so out the front door I went and ran upstairs next door to my cousin's house. These were the same cousins that moved in from Hanford about 3 years before, and they lived in a shotgun house that had a second story. I remember calling out my aunts' name as I got close to her front door. She came down the stairs and into my house and my cousin Carmen followed her and I just went about playing with my airplanes. That's when my cousin, who was maybe 1 year older than me, told me that my father was in an accident and would probably die. I had no idea what that meant. My Mom was still at work at the time in the cannery at Isleton and my aunt was taking care of me and my little sister. Eventually I did find out find out what death means, as those were dark days in our family as my dad did not survive the accident. My Mom went into a deep depression for weeks and we had lots of relatives stay over to help us through the transition. My dad had died returning from Isleton on the way to Pittsburg on that levee road and was involved in a head-on collision right before the Antioch bridge. He wanted to come home to take care of us and also was getting the keys on our first house that we were going to own. The collision was with a car that was carrying a boat behind it. He was 5 miles from our house, but he did not make it.

After the funeral my uncle, who lived on West 8th Street, had his oldest son Art move in with us. He was still in high school but took on that responsibility as he was very close to my father and used to work on cars with him. He kept an eye on all of us and he provided needed stability to our household for me and my 3 sisters and Mom. He was an athlete during high school and was on the undefeated Pittsburg Pirates football team in the early 60s. Eventually he was drafted into the Army and went to Vietnam. My Mom would send him tortillas and he would share them with his buddies and finally he returned and married his high school sweetheart, went to college and worked in banking and eventually became an athletic director and administrator for our local college. He was definitely was one of my family members who I have always admired. My oldest sister Irene, who used to care for me when Mom would be working, was popular, played clarinet in the Marching band and I can remember going to high school football games and seeing her perform. She always seemed so forward focused and knew she would leave town. Eventually when she graduated, she joined the Marines and would send my Mom postcards and letters while she was in the military. This was during the height of the Vietnam War and her duty was translating all the messages from the field. This deeply affected her I learned years later. Eventually she left the Marines and moved onto to San Diego where she married and had two children, one boy and one girl.

We eventually moved to another part of downtown to east 8th street next to the railroad tracks because we could not afford the rent on York Street after my dad died. So instead of going to our new house and starting a new life we moved on to start a new life without him. On 8th street we lived behind another house and away from the street which was alongside the railroad tracks of the Southern Pacific Railroad. I was in a new neighborhood trying to fit in, meanwhile my mother was still working in the fields trying to make ends meet for her 3 kids at home. It was not a totally safe neighborhood and one day that truth showed its ugly face. It was early Saturday morning and my little sister who was 6 years old bursts through the door crying and was trying to talk, but she was in shock. She had walked to the store around the corner to pick up something for my Mom. She told me in a later conversation what had happened. "I was walking back from the store and I noticed this man across the street looking at me. As I kept walking he kept looking at me and I crossed the street he followed me. I started getting nervous and started to skip because I was scared. As I turned and walked down our street, he grabbed me about two houses away from our house. I started kicking him and screaming until he finally let go and I ran through our alleyway to our house."

My Mom ran to her from the kitchen and held her to calm her down and my sister continued to cry as she tried to tell us what happened. She would put her hands over her face and stomp her feet as she said that a man who lived around the neighborhood had tried to kidnap her from the street as she was walking. She struggled and finally got away and ran as fast as she could to our house. My Mom quickly got on the phone and my uncle, and his older son, who lived across town quickly came and we got into his car and started looking through the neighborhood. My sister had told us who the person was once she was able to calm down and I knew who he was as he lived around the corner. We went down our street and around the corner but did not see him on the street, so we walked into the bowling alley around the corner from the house and there he was. My uncle told the manager what had happened, and we grabbed him, and we went to the police station. The police wanted my sister to go to the police station for a full statement however, the police department told us that since there were no witnesses and my sister was not harmed, and since the man had no priors no charges were going to pressed. We were told to stay away from the next street and if he did it again to let them know. It caused undue grief to the family for some-time, but we overcame it together, but I will never forget it.

Around the corner from our house was the Foster's Freeze where I ate my first fast food Chiliburger and had A&W root beers. The Pittsburg Bowl and Vogue Lanes Bowl were also near-by and I would keep score at both locations for 25 cents per game per bowler and as I got to know the owners, they taught me how to bowl and I used that as an outlet. My sister Gracie was a very good bowler and we would always compete against each other for the high score. She was able to overtake me because she was so determined and practiced and practiced and practiced. Our friend Broderick Perkins was on her bowling team and they used to play once a week. But Broderick really liked baseball. I remember Broderick getting frustrated many times when we used to practice because I could not pull the ball to left field as he pitched to me. He would become agitated time and time again and say to me;" Fernando if you don't pull my next pitch I am going to aim for your head." When Broderick was a senior in high school the coach would not let him play because he was slow on the bases and the coach would say "I only let my best players on the field." But Broderick would not give up. After High School he walked on and made the tryouts for the Diablo Valley Community College (DVC) and began hitting line drives from the first game he was in. He transferred to St. Marys College and got even better. He became a professional baseball player who played for the San Diego Padres and the Cleveland Indians. We had a lot of good baseball players in Pittsburg with multiple fields at the city and at our schools. I remember being on a team when I was about 14 with my friend James Bergins and he was on the pitcher's mound at the City Park with his Afro sticking out of his ballcap as he would look the opposing player on first base. I remember he used to tell me on the bench; "If he's on first base and he's gone, then he's gone." I used to go to Central Junior High and practice my hitting with my good friend Willie Herrera and try as I might, I still could not pull that ball as I was a natural spread hitter and hit it deep, but not to the left. My friends and I played on our neighborhood streets and. as we did not have a park close by, we played at the Veterans Hall parking lot in between East 8th street and East 9th street, made out of gravel, where we used to skin ourselves as we played tackle football and baseball. Chief would always want to call the plays and we would let him hike the ball because he was the most unathletic of all of us in that parking lot. We would laugh because Chief had always used to stutter and we would yell at him, come on Chief just say hike. At times we would help him out and finish what he wanted to say. But he knew his baseball and was a good friend. My friend Senaido Lopez, who would later be the first Puerto Rican Fireman in Contra Costa County, would always play with passion and call out fouls. My friend Peanut always wanted the ball, but he always would get irritated and start fights when he got tackled, so we changed his position. My good friend Oscar Quezada was the running back and he used to straight-arm all who tried to tackle him. Somehow I was made quarterback because I had the shotgun arm and could throw on a dime, maybe because I bowled so much. We would have to jump down at the end of lot down into the street to catch a long pass or fly ball on the dirt next the railroad tracks. Usually our friend Joey G. who lived downtown on Los Medanos Street was the guy I threw the ball to most of time. Joey was athletic and quick. He was a quiet guy but super competitive. We would always be on the look-out for the cars that would ramble down the street next to the railroad tracks. We all got hurt, we sometimes broke out in fights, we all laughed, and we were all friends in the prime of our life. We traveled on different paths as we grew up and apart. Joey G committed suicide, Oscar died due to complications after he fell as a result a drug overdose, Peanut died of cancer, Chief died of diabetes sometime after his legs were amputated. Some of the older guys in the neighborhoods were bikers and also part of the Street Life car club and they had cool customized low-riders and always kept them sharp as they rode them through the town. Those days will not be forgotten, and my friends will always be a shadow of my past. But I will always remember them, forever young. My cousins are also a big part of who I am. They may not know it, but its true.

TIME TO GO TO WORK

During the summers, when I as young as 5, I would go visit my cousins and my uncles would put me to work in the fields of the Monterrey peninsula in the towns of Castroville and Salinas. I can recall that one day I was taken out to pick boysenberries with my cousins. It was a hot day and we started out about 7 o'clock in the morning. We had to pick the boysenberries off the branches and lay them in this huge crate. Once the crate was full of boysenberries, they would punch a hole in our tickets so they could keep track of our pay. We may have been getting about 15 cents a crate. It would take about 20 minutes to fill that crate up. The kids would share filling up the crates as fast as we could. After a few hours of working and watching everyone I observed that there were little kids, grownups, and older adults doing this work. I then realized that this was not what I wanted to do for my life. I noticed that almost everyone who was picking the groups only knew Spanish. At about 10 AM on this day, I stopped stripping off the berries off of the branches and started eating my noon sandwich, which was kept in a brown paper bag. After being scolded by my older sister, I had to go back to work, but I knew that this was not the life I wanted even at the age of 9 years old.

I did not enjoy working in the fields as my skin would have rashes and I coughed all the time due to the pesticides being used. We would start before the sun would come up and with our pants and sleeves rolled up to keep out the chemicals that were sprayed all over the fields and on the crops. We would work all day till the sun came down. Breaks were few and far in-between and we at times earned about $5 a day after being in the dirt and in the heat of the sun, temperatures approaching 100 degrees and more. But we did what we were told and at the end of the day we would ride back to our cousin's house and make no mention of the work that we had just done. I knew I did not want to keep doing that work as I saw no end to it. When I was 16 I walked into almost every business in town and asked them if they would give me a chance to work. None was offered and I started spending more time outside the classroom. There was never any discussion about education in my home as the focus was having enough money to eat and if I could help my Mom I would.

I had ambition when I had no right to have to have it. I remember taking a push mower around multiple blocks and looking for work to pull weeds and mow lawns for less than $2 dollars to earn money to help my Mom. I was a newspaper boy, when newspapers cost a dime, and I always had the routes no one wanted in the bad side of town. At times some of the people would send their dogs at me when I came collecting for the cost of the newspaper. But I would go back and get my money and pay the newspaper.

Having a paper route seemed like a rite of passage in Pittsburg and after school I would hurry from Central Junior High and go to the Post-dispatch located downtown on Cumberland street and would meet the other newspaper boys. We would get our bundle for our routes from the circulation department and go outside next to the building and sit on the cement sidewalk and begin rolling up our newspapers as tight as we could and tighten the rubber bands around them as we put them in our satchels. We would compete to see who had the tightest newspapers and who could finish first and we would deliver the newspapers in our neighborhoods before 6 pm and try to deliver them next to the door for our customers as close as we could. There was homework to be done, but if there was light left we would play a little ball in the streets till the streetlights came on.

I recall one hot summer on the weekend, it felt about 95 degrees, I was walking on Montezuma Street and had been collecting for about an hour and I felt a sharp object on my back. I stopped and a voice said don't turn around; "Give me all the money you got." I had the money in my satchel along with the receipt book and I responded that I need to give the money to the Post-dispatch. The voice behind me said: "I don't' care, just drop your bag on the ground and don't look at me." Well I dropped the bag on the ground and started walking away and I turned my head and I could clearly see who the person was that was robbing me. I looked at my receipt book and estimated that he took about $19, and I needed to get it back. I finished collecting for the day about an hour later and I walked back up towards my house and neighborhood to East Street close to the Veterans Hall. I knocked on the door of a house I knew and was met by a friend of mine named Leroy from school. He said; "Hey Fernando, what's up? I replied to him, tell your brother David to give me the money he took from me when I was collecting or I'm going to tell your Mama." He was surprised, shook his head and yelled for his brother. His brother came to the door and Leroy stood there and looked at me and said; "You tell him." Well I did and I was not afraid, and I told him I would bring back my cousin Robert if he did give me back my money. He gave me back almost all of it and said he would give me the rest later, because he had spent some of it. I said I would be back the next day for the rest of it. I was naive but at the time I had no fear in the neighborhoods where I grew up. I listened intently to some of my teachers talk about potential all the time and that we needed to be achievers. I used my library card, took classes in speed reading, and I poured myself into learning. I was becoming aware and I wanted to learn about our US History and being Mexican in America and what that meant to so many. I knew my place was not where I was living but where I would be going.

CHOICES TO MAKE

I was a good student in primary school and elementary school and knew lots of kids in similar situations as mine. I used to joke an tell my friends I reached my peak in 3rd grade. But the times in the late 60s were full of lessons. A lot of my boyhood friends ended up in Juvenile hall where they did not learn to become model citizens. Some of my friends did not survive into adulthood as they got deeply into drugs, and violence. I was on the cross-country team in junior high, joined the chess team and tried my hand a playing trumpet. My friends and I would jump over the fences at the schools to play baseball on their good fields and look out for the police as we knew we would get into trouble. But the small town of Pittsburg always had places for us kids to enjoy. I and my friends used to go to the Boys Club where we played basketball, listened to music, joined in the arts and crafts, and listened to the music of the day. We would all go to the high school and jump into the Olympic sized pool when it got too hot in the summer. The carnival used to come into down and park right next to the park and we enjoyed our popcorn, the games and the rides on the Boomer-rang. We joined little league and played baseball as part of the summer leagues it seemed all day. For Christmas it seemed like everyone had roller skates, and that magic key, and we used to go to the skating Rink on the end of West 10th street. We would ride our bikes and have contests too see who had the loudest bike with playing cards tied to our spoke wheels rattling as we went through the neighborhoods. The river's edge was still not developed, and we would go downtown to the river and walk along the sandy beach and pick up seashells. I would go to the Green Onion record store, located across the street from the New Mecca café, managed by an old black man named Rufus. I would tell Rufus about Chicano music I knew about, Salsa, then later the soul bands like Tower of Power and of course Santana. Rufus was way way ahead of me. He would always school me and lay down Jimi Hendrix, Janis Joplin, Richie Havens and tell me about the old blues players, R&B and Motown. Rufus decided to start calling me Nando whenever I came into his store. I asked him why he wanted to call me Nando. "That's cuz only the famous have two syllables. Elvis, Ghandi, James Brown." He would pull out his dust cloth and dust down those 45s. Rufus would have his music blaring on his speakers outside the store any day he could get away with it. "Hey Nando, whats the word?" He would always greet me the same way. Rufus had connections in Detroit, and I heard that because of him a lot of famous artists played in Pittsburg. James Brown was his favorite.

Pittsburg was known for its sports teams, its reputation for having challenging schools, its steel mills, and for a hotbed of musicians for a small town and many have been recognized. From Pete Escovedo who continues to create that timbale sound to his daughter Sheila E who played with Prince. My friends Ramiro Amador, Leo Vigil and Leo Polvorosa, used to practice in the basement of my Moms house. Ramiro would later play over 20 years with Malo, Tierra, Jorge Santana, and other artists. Leo would play with major stars and create soundtracks. Mundi Orozco, Mr. Pittsburg, who played with the Midnight Devils, Diablo Sexto and help found the PHDs with Ramiro and Leo Vigil would blow his horn and provide offbeat humor. Curtis Ohlson who played his bass with Ray Charles and Buddy Rich. Rosie Gaines who was known as a vocalist and keyboard player with Prince. Art Addison was one of the best Saxophone and guitar players in the Burg and also played with groups in Hawaii. Sam Wesley, Gerald Glasper, Peter Riso are all well-known musicians. I would hang out with Benny Arroyo at his place and he would bring out his harmonicas and start playing the blues and music from the likes of Howling Wolf and J Geils. These are just a few of the outstanding musicians that are part of the Pittsburg Heritage. Jazz, Blues, Rock, Country, Funk; All the that the music that could be played, was played and is still being played. Pittsburg hosts an annual Sea-Food Festival and invites key performers and local musicians on that 3-day weekend in September. During the summer the downtown streets are closed to music and car shows allowing new Pittsburg residents to enjoy the gift of these talented artists. As I was growing up I would go to San Francisco and see these musicians perform and then later go to their houses as they hosted jam sessions with each other.

I would go lived a lot of music pouring out of poor families Growing up in the late 60s I was aware of the racial sentiment that was felt between the kids that were brought up downtown versus the kids that were brought up over the tracks. We seemed to overcome it because we would become teammates on the baseball, basketball and football teams. When Martin Luther King Jr was assassinated in 1968 the rage in the black community came to the surface and we had to deal with the aftermath of the race riots that occurred afterward in Pittsburg and was underscored in the country. For us that were not black we had been learning in our community about the injustices and beatings of blacks in the deep south and we talked about it. However, for my friends who were black it was a real part of their world everyday of their lives. I can clearly remember when they would walk on the street and see each other they would give each other a nod to that reality. As a Latino I felt the shadow of that racism.

In the late 60's and early 70s the Latino community in Pittsburg was active politically with locals becoming council members and Mayors. In those days many of the Latino people in town would go to the Centro on East 10th Street to get help for their taxes, paperwork for their work, look for help to secure a job, register to vote, and take classes to learn English or learn how to do secretarial work. The Mexican American Political Association (MAPA), the American GI Forum (AGIF) and the United Council of

Spanish Speaking Organizations were politically active in Pittsburg and helped shape many positive reforms and instill pride for so many in the community. There were numerous juntas in the restaurants, the park and the homes in the community when they wanted to effect change. These were the elders and they were the parents of the young Latinos who had not yet learned what it was to be a Chicano was about. Even still, the city council, school board, redevelopment agencies were not people of color.

I found that I thrived when I competed with my classmates while in school. I would stay up late into the night past 11 PM researching and writing book reports for my Science class. I was determined to get a better score than a good friend named Anthony Smith. During the early part of gym at Central Junior High School our teacher would ask us to run 2 laps around the fields that bordered the southeast part of our school. There was a baseball backstop at one end and at times some of the kids would try to sneak behind the backstop and hide to wait for the kids to come back around so that they did not need to do the required 2 laps as part of the full distance. Our gym teacher had a no-nonsense attitude, would grab a bat and run toward the backstop and begin yelling to get the offenders to run the full distance. I wanted so badly to come in first when we ran those laps. I would run to the front of the pack and run right behind this big kid, a friend of mine named Chris Jackson who was also on the track team, and try as I might I could never catch him as he was a foot taller, had huge quads, and was an athlete. But I enjoyed competing and my friends would be amazed at how I could keep up with these guys. My friend Michael Valle would say to our other boyhood friends;" Did you see Nando flying around the field?"

My friend Michael was the baseball player in school that all of us knew would go to the Majors. He always had a bat in his trunk because he was a star baseball player and was always ready to play. I was not as good a baseball player as him and he would spend time with me to focus on hitting the ball with the right balance so I could try out for the team. He was a catcher and as he grew up he made the high school team and when he was 16 he was being looked at by the San Francisco Giants and received a letter from Stanford showing their interest. He came by my house early in the morning one day and we talked for a few minutes, but he had to go see another friend of ours. Later that evening he was the victim of a knife fight at a party and died shortly there-after. It was a huge loss for his family, all of our friends, and the community. He was a good friend and I think of him often. Pittsburg was small in those days and Michael was known as a good kid with a bright future in baseball ahead of him. A baseball tournament, the Michael Valle Memorial Tournament, is held in his honor and support baseball scholarships that are given to young children.

TEATRO CARLITOS

My friends and I used to play close to the river's edge but one summer one of my good friends, Carlos Sanchez, drowned in the river. He was 15 and so was I. He was caught in the undertow and my friend Bobby Navarro tried to save him, but Carlos kept pulling them both under the water, and finally Bobby let go and tragedy struck. It was a tough time as Carlos was the kid that everyone thought would go far in life. He was quiet and persistent and had the greatest smile, had good grades and he made sure he made the right decisions. In the fall we founded a theatre group in his honor, and we gathered in the evenings to practice at the Centro, and I learned how to perform and acted for 2 years. We named our group Teatro Carlitos, named after Carlos, and It was modeled after El Teatro de Campesino a famous Chicano farmworker theater, founded by Luis Valdez in Delano during the early days of the farmworker movement. Luis Valdez is a Chicano playwright, actor, writer and film director now known by some of his works such as: I am Joaquin (1969), Zoot Suit (1981), La Bamba (1987), Coco (2017).

Teatro Carlitos was comprised of Mexican Americans and Filipinos from the downtown of Pittsburg, the neighborhood of Parkside, the orchards of Oakley and the farm camps of Brentwood. We would have lively discussions about the inspirations for the actos and discussed the Chicano movement, and our Identity. Bernice Rincon, my earliest mentor, a researcher and author would lead us in these discussions. Bernice Rincon was a highly educated Chicana feminist, ahead of her time, and activist. Our young director was Nick Vasquez who later went on to UCLA and became an educator in Southern California and followed by Hector Lopez from West Pittsburg who always seemed to be the philosopher of our group. With my good Alex Maldonado, whose family came from New Mexico, and Jose Aguilar, who family migrated from Mexico we continued to become educated about the Chicano movement as part of our youth. We were truly a dedicated Teatro. Sylvia Ramirez, who grew up in Brentwood in BG Camp with 10 brothers and sisters would capture the crowd in stunned silence as she performed "Soldado Razo" with many tears that flowed telling the story of a Mom and her son who had died in Vietnam.

We were truly La Raza and we were young ranging in age from 15 through 20. As the older members graduated from Community College and transferred to UC Davis, San Jose State or UCLA we would have new faces from our neighborhoods. We would perform in the auditoriums for high schools like Oakland Tech, the quad at colleges like Diablo Valley College, St. Mary's College, the theatres at Orange Coast College, UCLA and the California Legislature as we traveled throughout California. We would perform for La Raza at farmworker camps. As Luis Valdez said, "if La Raza won't go to the Teatro then the Teatro must go to La Raza" (Valdez,1990, ~Early Works pg 3). We would connect with Luis Valdez and his production company in the small town of San Juan Bautista located in the Monterey Coast. The essence of our work and the expression of Teatro was the actos as part of Chicano theatre. "Los actos son muy intersantes, chistosos, y representan la realidad de la vida del campesino" (Cesar Chavez). The actos reflected the daily strife and reality as felt by the farmworkers and parodied from the pain by the huelguista and how La Raza felt that the outside world viewed us. It was with pride that the Chicano theatre evolved as a different art form and continued to be a vital part of La Causa. The actos like "Los Vendidos," first performed at the Brown Beret junta in Elysia Park in East Los Angeles in 1967, and "Soldado Razo" first performed in Fresno at the Chicano Moratorium on the War in Vietnam in 1971, personified the humor and the soul of the Chicanos.

My younger sister, Gracie, was part of a Mexican Folklorico group of dancers who traveled throughout California and also practiced at the Centro along-side our Teatro. The young girls would recreate the elaborate flowering dresses worn in the different regions of Mexico and would be accompanied by young Chicanos in their pleated black pantalones and white or colored shirts and they danced to the songs and the stories of old Mexico. The Teatro and the Folklorico group supported each other with laughter, food, and music as we shared the common gathering place of the Centro. I was known as Smiling Faces as I was always upbeat and yes I did smile, but make no mistake, I worked hard on my work in the Teatro.

El Teatro Campesino continues to thrive in the small town of San Juan Bautista and located in an old warehouse. The Teatro continues to perform for the community with new works and celebrate with Aztec dancers. During the Christmas holiday they perform "La Pastorela" a musical retelling of the trek of the shepherds to Bethlehem to visit the Holy Child after a sign from the Angel of the Lord. Returning North from San Diego after taking care of my 90-year-old aunt I made San Juan Bautista my destination before returning to Pittsburg. I parked my car and slowly walked out in front of the old warehouse building of El Teatro Campesino. It was closed and I peered into the front box office and looked at the old playbills and before I left I decided to ring this small bell in front of the entrance. A Chicana answered and said 'Buenos Tardes." I was shocked anyone was there and I said. "Yo se que no estas abierto, pero se me puedes decir cuando vas esta abierto yo voy a venir patras." I was prepared to come back, but she said "Entra, Entra." I asked her how long she had been a caretaker for the Teatro, and she said; "Over 40 years." As I walked in I was stunned as I felt like I stepped back into the 60s with all the old posters of Cesar Chavez, pictures of the farmworkers, Cesar, Dolores, the march, the Chicano Moratorium, and signs that said 'Huelga, Huelga." I had an epiphany as I remembered working in the fields, boycotting during the grape strike and marching with the UFW. It was a long time ago, but yet here I was. There were pictures of the boycotts and playbills of Zoot Suit and I saw old Mexican colored zarapes and UFW flags. I walked to a small room and purchased an old copy of the Early Works-Actos by Luis Valdez. I slowly opened the paperback book and went thru the Actos that I was a part of when I was 16 and clearly remembered the characters:" Honest Sancho, Bernabe, Moctezuma and Miss Jiminez." I remembered Teatro Carlitos performing at St. Mary's College, Oakland Technical High School, UCLA. That was a long time ago. I thanked my host as I left the home of El Teatro Campesino in San Juan Bautista and told her I would be back to enjoy the festivals that they produce in town.

I remembered a time when our Teatro went to Southern California and were invited to perform with many other Teatros from the U.S and also the professional Teatro group called Los Mascarones. We performed outdoors to great applause and talked to Luis Valdez and the director of Los Mascarones about who we were and where we were from. I continued on my way back to Pittsburg and remembered those days long ago when I was beginning to really understand the injustice that was part of so many peoples' lives and not just Latinos.

SOCIAL AWAKENING

I continued my education in the streets of Pittsburg as a young teenager and I begin to absorb all the social injustices that I saw on television, newspapers, and in deeper reading at the library and in talking to those who have been impacted. I saw the coverage in the South as they tried to keep Black people from voting, the beatings and much more as they fought for their civil rights. I saw the killing of so many of our soldiers, and Vietnamese brought to my living room as part of the war, I saw the beginnings of the antiwar movement on local television as young college kids were protesting in Berkeley with the police beating on them to break up those who were against the war. I worked in the fields and was part of the hardships as farmworkers and heard the stories of us that were beaten by the police as they tried to organize for better working conditions and fair wages. Early in the 60s the schools still had not wanted to teach English as a second language to so many who needed it in their communities. I had some friends that were Native Americans and they told me their stories. Truly they were the only indigenous Americans. They would tell me that American Indians had been massacred from the late 1500s through the 1800s, but I did not see any of this taught in our schools. I would learn about the Trail of Tears and how our President Andrew Jackson really wanted to completely eliminate the Indians.

I found that discrimination and its injustice touched many lives, cultures and towns in the Delta. I learned that the town of Isleton where I started seemed like it was ground zero for racism. It surfaced in the 1860s, when the Chinese helped build the First Transcontinental Railroad. As the Chinese laborers began building the levees and the towns on the Sacramento River this racism was made manifest as part of the Chinese Exclusion Act of 1882, shutting down immigration but also naturalization. Then when the Japanese began to migrate and start their businesses in Isleton there would be mysterious fires who origins went undiscovered as the town needed to be rebuilt. The Japanese were then ordered by the government to be taken to internment camps during World War II and leave their homes and businesses in Isleton, many did not return. After this is when many Latinos, and some Filipinos moved to Isleton to work the farms and work in the canneries.

Pittsburg and our surrounding communities all the way to Stockton were on the fringe of the awakening to the injustices in the early 60s. Making not awakening, but the conversations that earlier were only silent whispers were now out in the open. I became more aware of the oppression by agriculture growers, personally, and the injustices of law enforcement as they looked upon farmworkers as property, the same as their farming tools and tractors. As first and 2nd generation Mexican Americans and with the continued oppression of Latinos in the United States the thoughts Chicano identity was memorialized in the poem I am Joaquin (19) by Rodolfo Corky Gonzalez. The Vietnam War, the deaths of Martin Luther King and Bobby Kennedy and the United Farmworkers striking for the right to organize, led by Cesar Chavez and Dolores Huerta (20), brought an awareness of the reality of life and oppression for those who were the poorest. I was intimately familiar with the life of the farmworkers as my family and I also worked the fields to feed our family and felt the pain of the hot sun, low wages and lack of respect by the growers.

In school as I was taught a lot about Euro-History and about the American Revolution. I went to the library to find out more about how the country was founded. I learned how the power of the 3 branches of government have been used and the wars that the US was involved in as a young nation. I found very little about the dark secrets that were part of our history. I also was very interested in our Presidents and the times in which they governed. I had idolized George Washington, Abraham Lincoln and Franklin Roosevelt as Presidents who had served during crucial times. But I also learned about Thomas Jefferson, Andrew Jackson, Woodrow Wilson and their views supporting racism once I really wanted to understand more than what was taught in school. Jefferson's "Notes on the State of Virginia" underscored his statements that Blacks were inferior. Andrew Jackson regularly put down anti-slavery demonstrations and his Indian Removal policies were really a mandate on genocide, in my opinion. Woodrow Wilson was an elitist and enjoyed showing "Birth of A Nation" at the White House which enabled the Klu Klux Klan. In 1848 Mexico was invaded and in 1898 Puerto Rico was taken over by our destiny to rule those people and eventually they have been treated as 2nd class citizens with laws that impoverish them..

John F Kennedy really seemed like he understood the injustices and worked to change the laws and ultimately Lyndon Johnson signed them into law in 1964. I can still recall the sadness my family and the community felt when John F Kennedy was assassinated in 1963. The war in Vietnam seemed a million miles away but it quickly seemed to come into our homes as my friends' brothers would not return when they were sent to fight in a place they had no place being. The Vietnam was escalated when Lyndon Johnson was President and the country began demonstrating against it as we would send over 500,000 men to fight in that war. With so much unrest in the country due to race, poverty and the war in Vietnam, President Johnson did not seek a 2nd term. After the election of Richard Nixon as President in 1968 the country was in an uproar about the war and Nixon did not trust the media and the people as well.

The year was 1969 and it was a watershed year for me, as well as the years that would come after, as I was becoming very aware of happenings outside of Pittsburg. The year before Martin Luther King was assassinated and Bobby

Kennedy was felled by an assassin's bullet. Neil Armstrong was the first man on the Moon, and I watched on television as he stepped out of his lander onto the moon with my Uncle Frank, the tank commander in WWII, in Castroville. It was the year of Woodstock in the little farm in Bethel, NY opened with by Richie Havens with "Freedom." Janis Joplin, Bob Dylan, Joan Baez, Crosby Stills Nash and Young Joe Cocker, Santana, and so many others played. The theme was love, not war and an estimated 400,000 kids from all over the US came with NY State having to close the Thruway, but yet they still came. The release of Abbey Road by the Beatles in the U.S, the Indians led by Richard Oakes occupied Alcatraz was significant to many. Some of my friends in the La Raza club from DVC were asked and went to help at the island as the Native Indians came off the island to fundraise for their cause.

In 1969 we had 543,000 military soldiers as a presence in Vietnam. The rise of Apple would be 7 years away and the IBM PC would take another 12 years before it was available. The shootings and the deaths of 4 young college students at Kent State in May of 1970, who were protesting the U. S. bombing in Cambodia, by the Ohio State National Guard further enraged many young Americans. The President showed no remorse and said he considered student protestors bums. The anti-war movement was in earnest and the peaceful Chicano Anti-War Moratorium in Los Angeles in September of 1970 tragically ended with the police beatings and the loss of Ruben Salazar, the first Chicano journalist who was reporting for a major newspaper. Gigi Fernandez, a friend from Pittsburg and Brown Beret talked about the day of the Chicano Moratorium. "After the police started beating the crowd I rushed to put small children, who were dressed for the festival, in a small bus and the police followed me and tear-gassed the bus and all the kids started crying and then the police knocked me out and a friend dragged me under a car for protection" (G.Fernandez, personal communication,9/6/2019).

When the Pentagon Papers were leaked in 1971 by Daniel Ellsberg, a Rand Analyst who had been to Vietnam and knew the truth, the American people were informed that the government had been involved in the war more deeply than we believed and even knew we were not going to prevail and yet they kept sending our young boys there because of political reasons. The President tried to stop the publication by the Washington Post and New York Times, however the Supreme court upheld the rights of the press as part of our First Amendment Rights outlined in the Constitution. Richard Nixon was first elected in 1968 with a promise "I pledge to you that we shall have an honorable end to the war in Vietnam." After so many lives were lost, with over 1 million Vietnamese and over 57,939 American young men dead or missing, the Paris Peace Accord was signed in 1973 to begin our exit from the war. The Watergate scandal begin by the Presidents men in 1972 and the subsequent uncovering of abuses of power, covered up by the administration and the President, led to the resignation of Richard Nixon in August of 1974. The country had changed from believing all that government had told us to a place where we wondered what would come next. How could you not be awakened to so much injustice? During this time there seemed to be so much chaos in our country because so many people felt like they were being treated as a sub-class as part of a ruling class strategy. Just like the years during the civil war the country was divided by those who believed in our government and those who wanted more truth and justice.

My wife's Aunt Jeanette is someone who I thought as a remarkable woman. She took her kids to hear a young black minister speak in Buffalo, the Reverend Martin Luther King, Jr. She joined the peace corps after her kids were adults. She got her bachelors' degree and teaching credential as well using public transportation. She became a mission and taught young kids in South Africa for over 20 years. She taught them English, Math and all the rest to get them ready for higher education. She was a stern, could not be pushed around and fought corruption even as local authorities took her money. She told me a story once about how the kids would walk about 5 miles daily over streams to get to her classes. The kids would have only a nub of a pencil and be grateful for that. She was there while apartheid was going on. The key for her was to feed the kids because that may have been the only meal that they ate all day. Once she hitch-hiked from South Africa up to the North. She was fearless.

My Mother-in-law Marguerite was priceless. She was a very smart and stern woman who valued responsibility. She told me a story once that when her husband said they were moving from Cape Cod back to Hamburg New York she said she did not un-pack for 6 months. My father-in-law at that time was getting out of the service and they had asked him to join the Green Berets. But he came home to his Mom and Dad instead. Marguerite and my father-in-law gave us all they could in ensuring we were all part of one family. I remember helping my father-in-law put up a deer stand one winter. Let me tell you as a kid from Pittsburg I was totally out of my element. Snow drifts reached over 7-foot high during some winters and my father-in-law would take his old tractor and plow around his house and for his friends in the neighborhood who needed help. They will always be in my heart.

My Tia Tula, my cousins Becky, Christina, Rose and Olgas Mom is someone who has always served the Lord. She was married to my Tio Connie until he passed away and she is can move on that dance floor. She has acerbic wit and always has made me laugh. When I was young she used to take me to the movies when I visited Isleton and stayed with them. She told me once that as she was growing up her family lived on a train as her dad worked for the railroad. But once he passed away they could no longer stay there, and they lived in a tent. I mean who lives in a tent. What a survivor. Luv ya Tia.

IF YOU"RE BROWN STICK AROUND

I will not outlive racism and discrimination as it was there when I was born, and it will be around after I am long gone. Discrimination has had an impact, but I will not let it define me. Being Poor has its advantages, if you can survive it. There used to be a saying when I was young; "If You're White Its Alright, If You Are Brown Stick Around, Yellow Is Mellow, and if You Are Black, Step Back." All of us that lived downtown seemed to understand what that saying was all about and who was saying it, but it was not our saying and we mostly ignored it. There was no discrimination, when it came to being part of poverty or poor. I was comfortable in my skin and did not feel different than anyone, but I knew others did not see it that way. Being a young man growing up in America, with Latino roots, often seemed like a paradoxical existence. There were those who insisted that we leave our roots behind us and to embrace the future. But there are also others who will not let us forget our heritage and use their bias to try to create a gap of inequality and oppression.

Mexico has had a long history of corruption and even after the Mexican Civil War which is also referred to as the Mexican Revolution which ended in 1920 it continued to serve the wealthy and not the people. Mexico's geography has the divided the country over the years and it was seen as a place where American Interests could profit. After the US Mexican war of 1848 when the US invaded Mexico, much of the Northern land representing 55% of Mexican territory was granted to the United States. Many of the existing native inhabitants were granted citizenship or were offered to return south to Mexico. Many stayed but many more moved to Mexico due to the racial policies by the US government and law enforcement of the times. The discrimination that existed before the war accelerated with many lynching's and shootings occurring as the newest inhabitants of that part of the country wanted control of the land (21).

There was a significant migration of these new US Citizens that resettled in Mexico. In the 1890s new industries like mining, agriculture and the railroads saw a need for cheap labor allowed the emigration of many Mexicans to go north and assisted by US agricultural contractors to disregard immigration laws. The amount of irrigated land in the early 1900s increased and so did the need for farmworkers. More than 25% of California's land mass is used for agriculture. The agriculture land in California stretches from the desert south of the Imperial Valley, through the south coast of Santa Barbara, thru the rich San Joaquin and Tulare Valley, the central coast of Monterrey, Contra Costa and Santa Cruz, to Valley of Sacramento and the North Coast of including Napa and Sonoma. The desert of town of Calexico next to the US border was the first town where widespread irrigation was implemented resulting in a huge increase of cotton, cucumber and lettuce crops and the influence of agribusiness owners.

The Mexican Revolution of 1910-1920 saw an increase in the immigration of Mexicans to the US to escape the violence with a peak of 100,000 new people per year in the 1920s. Latinos were segregated and forced to live in barrios with most Anglo Americans treating them as a sub-class. The Immigration Act of 1924 (22), which codified the Japanese Exclusion Act, established quotas, limited immigration from Asia and Eastern Europe exempted Mexicans from the new quotas established after lobbying by the South-Western Agriculture Industry. Proponents of the act sought to establish a distinct American identity by preserving its ethnic homogeneity. The act provided funding and legal instructions for the first time to courts of deportation for immigrants whose national quotas were exceeded. The Klu Klux Klan and Samuel Gompers, head of the American Federal of Labor, supported the new immigration Act. However, mob violence was commonplace against US Citizens of Mexican descent, as well as the Mexicans that were recruited to help the labor pool, in Texas, Arizona and California.

Olvera Street is considered is considered the birthplace of Los Angeles, around 1781, when Spaniards colonized this area, and where the indigenous people of the Tongva Nation originally lived. Today, Olvera Street is considered the heart of the Mexican culture of Los Angeles and comprise an area with monuments, restaurants, galleries, and people enjoy visiting the small stores and purchasing Latino themed goods. Each year several cultural activities take place here, including Dia de los Muertos, Mexican Revolution anniversary, Virgen de Guadalupe celebration, Los Tres Reyes, and more. Olvera Street is a short street, connected to a plaza and surrounded by murals, colorful stores and a permanent fiesta atmosphere. However, this location was used as a base for mass deportations by the government.

During the Great Depression the fears of job drove anti-discrimination to new heights with over 1.8 million people of Mexican descent were targeted and deported with possibly 60 percent of them being American Citizens, many of them born in the U.S to first-generation immigrants. These were the "repatriation drives," a series of informal raids that took place around the United States. For these citizens, deportation wasn't "repatriation"—it was exile from their country: (https://www.history.com/news/great-depression-repatriation-drives-mexico-deportation).

Existing Latino people were excluded from restaurants, movie theaters and schools and were forced to continue to live in segregated parts of the city of Los Angeles. Los Angeles was also populated with a diversity of people including among others; Filipinos, Blacks, Japanese. The fight for wages by the migrant labor force and the agriculture industry intensified between 1933-1939 resulting in over 180 strikes involving nearly 90,000 workers. (23) The

Zoot Suit riots of 1943, with tensions rising between Anglo Sailors and young Chicanos in Los Angeles who were viewed by police as criminals allowing for the beatings by US Sailors showed another example of discrimination. In 1946, almost a decade before the Supreme Court in the Brown vs Board of Education ruling ending segregation in schools based on race, a ruling in California district court: Mendez VS Westminster, outlawed school districts discriminating against Mexican American students and violating their constitutional rights.

In 1942 the bracero program was signed into law which was an agreement between the US and the Mexican government for the use of manual laborers, also described as guest workers for public consumption, from Mexico. Due to the numerous irregularities and corruption there were many strikes by Bracero workers due to wages not being paid properly, poor living conditions, harsh working conditions, and lack of supervised inspections At its peak 62,000 braceros per year came to the US to support farm labor with the initial act expiring in 1947. US Citizens of Mexican descent served in both World Wars and in Korea but as the Korean War ended in 1952 anti-Latino discrimination continued.

In the 1940s the Mexican American community lived in the hills of what was called Chavez Canyon and lies north of Los Angeles. Originally the land was purchased in the 1830s by Julian Chavez a local leader and was settled due to the housing discrimination that existed in Los Angeles. The barrios of Bishop, La Loma, and Palo Verdes were distinct communities within the hillsides where families lived and created neighborhoods and businesses. However, in the late 40s and early 50s the City of Los Angeles wanted to take over the properties of the community and ultimately forced the families, using the police as enforcers, filing the takeover through eminent domain. Initially developers paid owners what was needed to have them move and then offered less and less to other owners of the property. People were taken out after being handcuffed and dragged from their homes in protest as bulldozers began knocking down the houses where these innocent Latinos lived and raised their children. Promised relocations to new developments were never built as they forced the families out of their homes and neighborhoods. In 1958 Los Angeles taxpayers approved a baseball referendum transferring the land to the Dodgers to build their stadium.

The Agriculture industry still needed workers to work their fields and the Bracero program was extended multiple times, led to the establishment of the H-2A Visa program, with the official termination in 1964. The termination laid the foundation for a new generation of farmworkers and ultimately led to the creation of the National Farmworkers Union and ultimately the United Farmworkers Union led by Cesar Chavez and Dolores Huerta. In the Latino communities it was common to accept the way the families were being treated with fear of reprisals and the history of being deported out of the country still part of the culture. Spanish was expressly rejected to be spoken in schools with no bilingual education. This was common all over the country through the 1960s. I am underscoring the times for Latinos and others and we should be careful not to fixate on the past but we should not deny it as it has a way of sometimes re-inventing itself especially when others have unfounded fears and look to find fault and follow leaders who divide and not unite. Because Mexico is situated next to the United States with its Southern Border, and its population of poor coming over to the US legally and illegally, these immigrants have long been an easy target of laws that are continually overturned as unconstitutional. History has shown that even if comprehensive reform that is fair and just is passed by the Congress it will take many years for equality to be felt by all.

CESAR CHAVEZ

Cesar Chavez was an American labor and civil rights leader who with Dolores Huerta co-founded the United Farm Workers Union (UFW). As a farm-worker Cesar Chavez was directly impacted by the mistreatment of farmworkers as they worked to earn living wages for their families. He had worked for ten years with the Community Service Organization as an organizer for that civil rights group and traveled throughout California in support of workers right. In 1962 the UFW was formed and when the Filipino American farmworkers initiated the Delano grape strike in 1965 to protest unjust wages and poor working conditions under the leadership of Larry Itilong and the Filipino Manongs. Chavez provided the leadership for the Mexican American farmworkers to support the Filipino strike and unify.

In the 20s and 30s, 100,000 Filipino men flocked to America and became the migrant workers and followed the group cycle over the West Coast (Sandoval, C. Oct 17, 2018. Newsy; How Filipinos Shaped an American Labor Movement In the 60s). After a record fall harvest in 1965 the farmworkers demanded representation by a Union, and many were beaten by police and arrested as they picketed In September and the workers in Delano walked out of the fields for better wages and began the Delano Grape Strike It would last for 5 years.

On March 17 1966 Cesar Chavez and a few farmworkers, both Filipino and Mexican Americans, started their walk to the Capital in Sacramento, to bring visibility to the Grape Strike as they marched for civil rights of the workers, organized and fighting for the right to have at least minimum wages, fair treatment, free from scabs and for the right to have a contract that outlined what the growers and the workers would agree to. Day by day under the intense heat the farmworkers walked, even as their shoes fell apart and would be joined along the way with over 15,000 joining the march. From the 30s through the 70s the growers had the power and the guns and would use scab workers to break strikes and jail the farmworkers as they toiled in the fields day after day when they asked to have the rights that belonged to other Americans. Contractors would hire their families with children as young as 3 and grandfathers and grandmothers to work in the fields and would make them pay for water and the use of sanitary facilities from their meager pay as they worked from sun-up to sundown.

Later the UFW encouraged all Americans to boycott table grapes as a show of support with the strike lasting for 5 years until an agreement for the first collective contract for the UFW growers was signed. These activities led to similar actions in Arizona and Texas and the Mid-West United States. In the early 1970s the UFW organized strikes and boycotts. My mother's cousin, Herlindo Reyes, who worked at the Social Security office in Tijuana, established a health care plan with Cesar, and traveled for 2 years to the fields to sign up the workers at the halls, for farmworkers families who lived in Mexico.

As a young child I was used to seeing the produce that was picked by the farmworkers and was brought into the cannery on a daily basis from the farms on the delta. Later as I turned 4 when I visited my relatives I was asked to help with the work of the families in the Delta and Monterrey. In the adjoining towns of Brentwood, Oakley and all the way thru Stockton many of my friends and their families would work the fields to support their families. Many would travel from the Imperial Valley, the Central Coast and San Joaquin Valley picking cotton, boysenberries, loose leaf lettuce, tomatoes, among others. I was exposed to the hardships by the workers that I worked alongside. I was asked to roll-up my pants and sleeves to keep out the DDT and other pesticides that I would come in contact with from the dusk early in the morning till the sun went down. I provided with a small brown paper bag to fill with fruit and a sandwich to quench my hunger during the day. Water would be provided, if it existed, by the growers on the farm. I made less than 3 dollars a day working the fields along with the other children with the adults making about 10 dollars a day.

Usually there were no facilities to relieve yourself and you would have to go far out into the fields to take of that business. When farmworkers were being organized the growers would disperse them so that they would not collectively hear the injustices that were being discussed. I became aware at a very young age what the injustices of the farmworker's families were facing. I listened as the seeds of discontent led to the movement of the UFW. Cesar Chavez came up from Delano and spoke in the basement of the St. Peter Martyr Church in Pittsburg. He let the locals know what was coming. Dolores Huerta galvanized the workers from Stockton to the Delta for the upcoming Huelgas and Boycotts that were going to be part of our lives. The grape strikes and boycotts lasted from September 1965 until July 1970. The local families in Pittsburg, Stockton, Brentwood, Oakley made bread, soup, and tortillas for the workers and families who would be going on strike. Cesar went south to Castroville to rally the workers there and across the Monterey peninsula. Cesar and Dolores went all across California and galvanized the country and showing the poverty that farmworkers faced daily and only asked for the rights that all Americans had for fair wages, living conditions and to be treated humanely. As Cesar said; "It's not about the grapes, it's about the people, the seniors working in the fields and the young kids who had nothing.

CHICANOS AND OTHER MOVEMENTS

The Chicano movement of the 1960s, also called the awakening, was the civil rights movement to extend the rights of Mexican Americans with the goal of seeking empowerment as part of the American Culture. Young Chicano activists stood on shoulders of UFW leaders for farm-workers' rights, enhanced education, fair housing, political and voting rights and affirmation for ethnic Latinos. There were many in the Latino world who looked as these new Chicanos with disdain as they wanted to separate themselves with the movement. The conflicts, especially in the Los Angeles area with the LAPD, helped Mexican Americans develop a new consciousness and solidarity of purpose to help reduce the sub-class perception of its people. Chicanos were derived from all walks of life in the American experience from labor workers, to educators, to scientists and lawyers. The League of United Latin American Citizens (LULAC) was formed in 1929 to reduce discrimination and the American GI Forum (AGIF) established in Texas is a congressionally chartered Hispanic Veterans and civil rights organization founded in 1948.

After World War II many veterans of Mexican descent were denied medical services by the Department of Veterans Affairs and the AGIF fought for those services, educational desegregation and voting rights. AGIF and LULAC helped win a Supreme Court verdict in 1954 Hernandez v Texas after a Mexican farmworker was convicted by an all-white biased jury. Texas had continually excluded Mexican Americans from serving as "jury of peers" and the Supreme Court ruled that that they were discrimination was proven and that they and all other racial or national groups had equal protection under the 14th Amendment. The Mexican American Political Association (MAPA) was created to strategy plan for direct electoral politics and became the voice of the Mexican American Community of California. These groups participated to root out discrimination and press for equality. The Chicano movement has continued to evolve to support increases for political representation, inclusion in major media and educate Latinos about their voice and power through voter registration projects and local elections.

The Chicano movement was front and center and oppositional against class repression and galvanized many of its people to support walkouts, boycotts, and gaining reforms including implementation of bilingual education. Los Angeles was the melting pot of Latinos who were forced to life constantly repressed by the education system, the judicial system, the abject discrimination on housing, and the unfair policing of its families by the LAPD and Sheriff's department. Students on the Eastside participating in blow-outs, walking out on classes to demand an end to unequal education. In some cases, the doors of the schools were padlocked so students could not leave and demonstrate. In 1970, the National Chicano Moratorium, an antiwar demonstration drew hundreds of thousands, resulted in the death of Ruben Salazar a noted journalist of the LA Times by the law authorities.

I went into the military service as a proud Chicano and American who would not tolerate racial insensitivities by those I worked with and I grew to understand how to educate those who had no context or were mis informed. There is an older generation that never embraced Chicanismo (27) and in many cases assimilated into the fabric of society. There were many reforms that were successful, and Latinos began to organize and vote in elections to enable changes. Many of my Chicano friends over the years became teachers, administrators, engineers, became federal agents and ran and won seats for political office. However, the gains did not come easily. As the years passed many of the young activists realized the gains that they worked for and assimilated into society as contributing citizens while trying to keep their culture alive.

I reflect on those days because they are a part of our culture's history in the United States and re-enforced identity and empowerment. We do not want to fixate on the rear-view mirror otherwise we will drive off the road. However, we should always ensure that we do not forget those who survived those hardships and those who gave so much of themselves so that we could have the opportunities to move forward and succeed. The responsibility of being a Chicano is greater than oneself and extends to the children and grandchildren of those who worked for fair treatment and the rights of citizenship and ensuring that our cultural heritage does not disappear.

The young Chicanos in our community formed the Brown Berets after many of my friends came back from Los Angeles and saw and felt first-hand how the police interfered and many times beat young Latinos that asked for better schools and demonstrated against the racism in schools and employment in sections of town, which would not employ Latinos. I was young and was becoming aware of this repression and we worked to help those families that were affected. We participated in leading walkouts in our schools, demanded bi-lingual education, provided security for protestors, and participated with organizers to support the boycotts at the national grocery chains against the growers. One of my good friends, Fidel Huerta, who is the son of UFW Co-founder Dolores Huerta, attended Los Medanos Community College before he transferred to UCLA and become a doctor and ultimately was Cesar Chavez personal physician and whose job was to keep him alive during his last fast. He later became director of the Kern County Medical Center.

The Chicano movement extended beyond the SF Bay Area with Latinos in Arizona, New Mexico, Texas, Colorado and across the United States. On March 20th, 1969 there was a walkout In Denver, Colorado.

The high school walkouts were considered one of the largest and most violent as police in riot gear ran over the protestors with their batons and arrested many. The walkouts were planned to demonstrate discriminatory practices in the schools, inadequate education, and advising Latinos to join the military. Chicano Youth Liberation Conferences in 1969 and 1970 brought together large numbers of Chicano youth from the Southwest, the Northwest, and the Midwest, as well as Puerto Rican youth from the Midwest and East Coast. There are many Chicanos who lament the days of the past and wonder what the future holds once the OGs are gone. This is especially true for those of us who have reaped the gains of educational attainment and continue to be activists. Educating young Latinos on the history of the movement, its effects, current discriminatory laws being enacted, and how they can be impacted is a goal of the OG's of the Chicano movement.

During these times some of my friends were also part of the Black Panther Party. The Black Panther party with leaders such as Bobby Seale, Stokely Carmichael, Huey Newton, and Angela Davis fought against the oppression of blacks in our communities and their goal was to end brutality against blacks in the city of Oakland. A good school friend of mine, named E.C.

was a part of the Panthers and he would tell me about why he was in the Panthers. He was from Richmond and was feared as much as he was respected. He would tell his close friends; "Don't Mess with the Brain." That was a nickname he liked to use for me as I helped him in school and told him about the Chicano movement and told me about the Panthers. The Black Panthers had a Ten Point program outlining self-defense and their policy for Black Equality and Compensation. In 1967 they demonstrated in the California Capital, fully armed as was their right, and protested against pending gun control legislation as part of the Mulford Act, as it was directed against Panthers. The NRA actually supported this gun control legislation and it was signed into law by then govenor Ronald Reagan.

The Black Panther Party who also provided community health care services, food to the poor, shoes to those who had none were targeted by the FBI as dangerous group. The book Soul on Ice by one of their members, Eldridge Cleaver, outlined the outrage that was memorialized in the black community. In time the group dissolved as the leadership was jailed, were killed or moved on. But the Black Panther Party was more than just militancy as they were focused on the poverty that existed in communities. From 1969 thru the early 70s they instituted the "Free Breakfast for School Children "program feeding tens of thousands of hungry kids. They organized and setup legal clinics and medical outreach clinics for the poor in the communities in which they were organized. Many of these programs were then copied throughout the country and the Federal Government began institutionalizing them with funding.

I have many friends who are of Puerto Rican descent. They are proud of their unique heritage and these families were close knit in Pittsburg. As I discovered Puerto Ricans are American citizens, yet they still struggle with their own indigenous background. The US invaded Puerto Rico in 1898 and were involuntarily taken over by the U.S. Many migrated to New York City and Chicago and faced oppressive conditions. A group called the Young Lords from Chicago inspired by the Black Panthers and evolved to work for social justice for Puerto Ricans, self-determination, and have a political voice. The citizens of Puerto Rico on the island to this day still cannot vote for president and have no authoritative voice in congress to press for their rights.

Over the years the town of Pittsburg and its school district has been progressive when it comes to equality due to its diversity of citizens. The

84

Pittsburg Unified School District instituted Bilingual education before it was mandated and funded by the federal government. I may not have had the benefit of bilingual education when I was young, but the citizens of the town pressed for this to be included in the curriculum. Rudy Rodriguez a lawyer, who was a key member of the Mexican American Political Association (MAPA), Gigi Fernandez of the Brown Berets and Ernie Quintana prepared the case to the school district and Pittsburg decided to include this as part of their curriculum.

The City of Pittsburg has evolved and has included Latinos and Blacks in positions including School Board, City Council and Mayor. Streets and parks are named after prominent citizens regardless of their race or ethnicity. There were additional cases in the country which tried to deny equal protection for Latinos. The Supreme Court ruled in 1982, in the case of Plyler vs Doe, held that a Texas statue which withheld state funds for the education of children that were not legally admitted into the United States, violated the Equal Protection Clause of the 14th Amendment. This case was successfully litigated, among other others, by Peter Roos, the director of the Mexican American Legal Defense Foundation (MALDEF). It was a victory for civil rights for everyone. The Courts held that the illegal aliens of today may be the legal citizens of the future and they cannot be denied the protections as affirmed in the Constitution. There were many activists who made a positive difference for the Latino Community. Joel Garcia is one such contributor, he helped as founder of MECha. MEChA is a student organization in many colleges that promotes higher education, culture and history. He also founded Clinica De La Raza and Legal Services for La Raza. He is unwavering and once said as he retired from his organizations; "a person can retire from a post, a position, a board, an organization, but you can never retire from a cause."

The schools in Pittsburg continue to support programs for Immersion and English as a second language for its students, however there is much work to do as our graduates continue to score in the 20th to 25th percentile in English and Mathematics compared to the 80% in other school systems in Contra Costa County. The Latino community in Pittsburg continues to evolve as families from Honduras, Guatemala, El Salvador, Nicaragua continue to settle in Pittsburg, Antioch, Oakley and Brentwood adding to the challenge for educators. There is more work to do.

FROM SCIENCE FICTION TO THE FUTURE

As a young child I would go the Vogue Theater on Central Avenue in Pittsburg and on weekends I would watch Flash Gordon, a spaceman who used to travel to planets to save those worlds. That inspired me to learn about rocket ships, space, and the future of space travel. I recall being totally consumed by United States space program with the goal of landing a man on the moon. I would read as much as I could about it, started to learn about astronomy, about the math involved and dreamed of being an astronaut or an engineer. It never occurred to me, until much later, that if I worked on my education, I could become an engineer.

In my little cocoon of a family, at least for my mom, she never thought I could do something like that.

Growing up, technology was not a big part of anyone's lives except for the military and government. Everyone worked on their own cars, used a rotary telephone, had 3 television channels, and used paper to send letters and pads to keep notes. I found out early that because my eye was not 20/20 I could be not considered to be part of that astronaut program I would watch shows like the "The Time Tunnel, and Star Trek" and imagined what it be like to be a scientist or being on a spaceship. I would go to the library and read reference books on the space program, books on Albert Einstein, Thomas Edison and Nickola Tesla, and checkout sci-fi books with authors like Jules Verne who wrote From the Earth to the Moon, 20,000 Leagues under the Sea, HG Wells who was a visionary who wrote: The Time Machine, War of the Worlds, The Shape of Things to Come.

However, it was a chance meeting in my uncle's garage that raised my curiosity to the next level.

My uncle worked the line at a local canning company in Pittsburg and was responsible for ensuring that the line continued to operate at full production during his shift, he worked on cars for a hobby, but he had other interests as well. On one hot summer's day when I was 10 years old, I found him inside of his garage immersed in fixing televisions from the neighborhood and I can remember the electronic instruments he had at hand to help him. I was surprised that he had the knowledge to work and repair these televisions and asked him how he learned to do that as I knew he never went beyond the 8th grade. He pointed to the top of a bookcase on the wall of his garage to all the slim books and told me he knew that the televisions kept breaking down and he taught himself electronics so he could repair them. I asked him If he could teach me. He told me to take some books, go read them, and come back to ask him questions and he would quiz me. I then had a weekly ritual during that summer of taking 5 books home returning to his garage where he would begin to test my knowledge and mentor me on the instruments that he used as tools to calibrate and solve problems. I learned about electronic theory, diodes, capacitors, ohms law, tubes and how circuits worked together and many other advanced concepts. A few times he let me do some work with him. This was a whole new world of knowledge for me and I picked up other books at the library on electronics and learned about Edison, Tesla, Marconi while my friends were starting to look for trouble and hanging out with the older kids.

I was able to work with my uncle on building some television sets and working with him doing measurements. When I took an electronics course in junior high school my teacher, Mr. Caldwell, who was also a Major in the reserves, was surprised at my core knowledge and he continued to help me develop my interest. I used to try to stop my classmates who used to have fun throwing old vacuum tubes out of the 2nd story window and watch to see how they broke once they hit the ground. Mr. Caldwell would command all my attention and tell me about the early history of electronics, how it was applied on television, cars, refrigerators. I would be fascinated as he talked about the future of computers and how they would change our world in ways we could not imagine and be needed for the space program for flights to the Moon, to Mars and back. I would go with my friends to see our high school football team and in one hand I would always have a book and they would laugh and wonder what I was always reading about.

I did not know it then, as a young child growing up, but one day I would be the Chicano from the neighborhood traveling on the waves of the oceans having the knowledge and skills to maintain computers that had been designed to do more than just play the game of pong. Years later I would be working at the IBM facility in Owego New York where many of the systems of the Space Shuttle were being developed. As I watched the television science fiction show Star Trek in 1966, when I was 11 years old, I never imagined I would be on the USS Enterprise. I will always remember how much my electronics teacher sustained my interest, but I will always treasure that my first teacher who paved the way for me to learn electronics and later computers was my Uncle Art, a proud man who worked the line at the canning plant. Thank You Tio !!!

LEAP OF FAITH- IN THE SHADOWS OF GREATNESS

As a young man in my small town I did the normal things kids do, mowing the lawn to earn money, having two paper-routes, one in a very bad part of town. I could never land a job in town, even as a stock boy at a furniture store. But the training and experience I received complex computer systems and serving on the USS Enterprise would change the course of my life.

Because I scored so high on my Naval Entrance exams, and other tests my processors had faith that I could excel as part of the Advanced Electronics program, but I was not sure what I was expected to learn and how long it would take. I was initially trained on a core electronics in San Diego for weeks then I was sent to be trained at Mare Island, California at a Navy base where submarines used to be refitted and where the Nuclear Program training was also based. The data systems school was very difficult with core training lasting 6 months additional specialization training lasting another 6 months. I worked with the training program 5 days a week and at times on weekends, learning discrete electronics, architecture design, Boolean mathematics, digital computers, programming, and systems integration. Boolean Algebra, developed by George Boole (30), was the basis of digital computer design and was developed in the late 1800s. I was able to pick up the concepts quickly and helped young recruits from Nebraska, New York, and Colorado when they had problems. I was a natural in forensics and this helped me understand troubleshooting theory and modeling. The Navy wanted to ensure that I was the best before they sent me to work with others who were also trained on real time computers that tracked jets, submarines and integrated with 3D radar systems. I can recall a time when we had to perform programming in machine language, with a transportable computer, the Univac Digital Trainer, and if the ships were doing radar testing our programs would be wiped out and we would have to start over. Later we learned how to use compilers as we programmed in different languages. I was initially trained to maintain, diagnose, program, and repair computers initially designed by Seymour Cray.

The NTDS (Naval Tactical Data System) computers that I was trained on were originally designed by Seymour Cray, the Father of Supercomputing (28). Before they were deployed for production Univac redesigned the using silicon transistors but keeping the core Instruction set so that the original programs would continue to run on both. Seymour was a brilliant engineer and worked on the crypto systems while he was in the service and designed the first commercial digital computer. He was a member of the Sperry Rand Univac division in his early years and later was the key designer for Computer Data Corporation and designed the first supercomputer, the CDC 7600. He founded Cray Research and his new innovative designs were bought by the Department of Defense, Universities, the National Security Agency and other secretive organizations. His first computer, named the Cray-1, was purchased by the Los Alamos Laboratory in 1976. He was once asked what tools he used to design his early work and he replied: "pencil and paper." He had designed the earliest digital computer in his head, with a pencil and paper drawing upon Boolean Algebraic mathematics created in the 1850s by George Boole. Boolean mathematics has been used as the fundamental basis of computer science digital design logic, programming and statistics. In Boolean Algebra you learn about the concepts of duality in digital circuits and is used to prove various theorems. The circuits in digital computers follows the mind and the use of Boolean Algebra deals with the solving of multiple various variables however always understanding that the truth set only contains two values as part of the sets being calculated. The logic is considered binary in its purest form and can be equated to resemble 'truth' or 'false' represented by a 1 or a 0.

Designing and manufacturing computers involves multiple disciplines and different high-level skills from Electronic Engineers, Computer Scientists, Mechanical Engineers, Integrators and many others. Seymour Cray was ahead of his time as he would create the overall design, the logic to support the design, research and use the components available, and build the circuits. Cray would create the programs, by himself and do quality assurance testing. He would use teams of mathematicians and engineers to validate his designs. He also created designs knowing that components would fail and created backup circuits to bring his vision to practicality and created the operating system software to allow them to run as he continued to show his genius in that field. At one time in later years Cray walked into a roomful of design engineers who were in heated discussions about one facet of perfecting a control scheme as part of an advanced design. Cray asked what the problem was, and then went to the whiteboard and quickly laid out his thoughts on their problem and walked out. They were astonished as Cray quickly designed the entire control scheme with parallel circuits used for fault control, in ten minutes, on the whiteboard. While IBM and other early computer companies built their systems with CPU speed in mind, Cray designed his computers to go twice and at times 4 times as fast and even measured the length of wires to maximize the efficiency how long it took a signal to go from output to input and how the electronic signal would degrade. In later years at Lawrence Livermore National Laboratory I was part of a team that worked on a micro-multiplexor design solution that was delivered to Cray.

Howard Hughes (29), the owner of Hughes Aircraft, was an innovator in his time, and under his direction his engineers were considered some of the most advanced in the world. His Engineers designed the tactical display systems and the 3D Radar Integration Systems that I became an expert on. Howard Hughes built and flew the fastest planes in the world. His company was involved in aerospace, defense, electronics, mass media, manufacturing, oil drilling and medical research. His scientists created the first geo-stationary satellite and at one time 90% of the satellites orbiting the earth were from Hughes Aircraft and were used for public communications crypto communications, high speed navigational, and many other purposes. Howard Hughes was a futurist and his teams worked on light-weight materials for aircraft design which created the Spruce Goose the largest plane ever built with a wingspan of over 300 feet. He was involved in television, making movies and built very specific factories and hired women to important and highly paid positions in his company. He contracted a disorder and felled by mental illness due to the result of a plane crash that he was piloting when he was very young.

So, before I reached the age of 20, I was in the shadows of Seymour Cray, Howard Hughes, and George Boole. I was trained and working on the electronics, using the digital mathematics laws and the programming, and the analog and the digital technologies for these complex systems and supporting their use and processes in real-time on an Aircraft carrier that carried 100 jet aircraft and 5,000 men.

I noticed that I was the only Latino assigned to our Combat Computer Systems team.

I am glad I did not get that job at the furniture store.

SOUTH CHINA SEA AND BEYOND

When I first arrived onboard our ship was on station on the South China Sea. The South China Sea in in the Pacific Ocean abutting the Philippines, China and extending to Malacca and the Taiwan Straits, an area of approximately 2.1 million miles. Aircraft Carriers do not run themselves and we had trained guys at every rate; Electronics Tech, Enginemen, Aircraft Maintenance, Air Department (Launch/Recovery), Communications, Medical, Engineering, Operations, Reactor, Supply, Weapons, Snipes and many others. I used to enjoy coming on deck as we did Underway Replenishment at sea with a ship moving at our same speed and maneuvering the winds and the waves right next to us tethered with huge cables and we brought provisions onboard. I made many friends and one was Sam Plumlee. Sam was an Irishman from New Mexico with huge strong arms who had worked underground in the mines in Carlsbad. He introduced me to country music as he played country guitar late at night after shifts and I would sneak up with him to the 0-15 level, 15 levels above the flight deck, as he was assigned to be the Captains cook and he would make these awesome steak sandwiches about 11 at night.

Beyond the danger of flight Operations, which we did daily and at night, always on our minds was the threat of Fire. I can recall on the ships 1MC speakers I would hear a southern voice blaring for all to hear; "There's a Fire, There's a Fire at 05-26-3-5. Again, there is a fire at 05-26-3-5, please stand aside, Nucleus Fire Party will provide". That fire was close to the front of the ship, 5 decks below the flight deck next to the Liquid Oxygen plant, which was highly combustible. If the plant caught on fire it would explode and create such heat that surrounding compartments could begin to superheat. A fire on deck which started with a rocket explosion as was part of additional bomb explosions and leaving jet fuel to burn below decks. A total of 18 explosions occurred, blowing 8 holes into the flight deck and beyond. The Nucleus Fire Party were highly trained, and they would run as a group with their gear, up and down the ladders and through our narrow corridors, in their RED colored uniforms, and everyone would get out of the way quickly with our back against the walls in many cases. At that moment they were the most important people on our ship.

Our computer space was crowded with the various computers which were designed for specific programs, crypto communications equipment, integration systems, 3D radar interfaces, cables and other specialized equipment. When I walked up into the Combat Information Center, which many times was lit up with red neon lights, with all the Display Consoles, Maps, Electronic ID rooms, it was like walking into a different world. Working 12-hour shifts at sea, allowed me the time to learn many of the different systems that were used to support our Combat Information Center. Sperry Univac had the contract for the various computers, and Hughes Aircraft had the contract for the display and 3D Radar integrations, Collins for radio systems and Raytheon for the radars. Command and Control, Display systems, Electronic Warfare, Navigation and Air Traffic control systems all were part of our responsibility. Our Beacon Video Processing (BVP) system utilized the Identification Friend or Foe (IFF) technology which was later adapted with transponders for commercial aircraft. The BVP provided automatic tracking of friendly aircraft, unknown aircraft, correlated their signatures of range and bearing and provided digital processing attributes and showed the Air Controllers who was in the air, how high and how fast they were traveling.

As we came off station in the South China Sea, we ported at NAS Cubi Point in the island of Luzon in the Philippines. Once in port we would take taxis from the ship over to the main base and walk through the gates to the town of Olongapo. The town of Olongapo was a rest and relaxation way station for the soldiers and military men so it was very different than what I ever experienced. After our morning muster on the ship, scheduled maintenance and cleaning detail we were allowed to have time off after 1 PM. For those who did not have the duty, watch detail, we got ready with our civilian clothes and got on the cars that took us from Cubi Point to the Main base adjoining the front gate. Some of us went to the base bowling alley, the Navy Exchange to purchase goods to send back home, and other on base facilities. Most of us made our way to the main gate to begin to find a way to spend the money that we had earned and saved which we were out at sea.

We had to walk across a bridge where natives would be in small pongas (carved out wooden boats holding 6 people) with small netted baskets and swimming in very brown unsanitary waters waiting for coins to be dropped. One time one of our guys fell into the that water and he had to be fished out and they kept him in quarantine as they filled his body with different medicines to ensure he would make it. The town itself was lined on both sides with bars and Neon Lights that would blaze at night. Natives would be selling barbecue meat on the street and everyone would be coming at you to be your friend, to sell you something, and take your money. I learned how to drink San Miguel beer, eat gorges of rice at a setting and what we called monkey meat. It was not real monkey, but we were not sure what it was. We would be entertained from the time we set foot into town and at the end of the evening, before curfew would come at midnight we would head back to base or if we could not make it in time we would look for a place to stay inside till morning. You would see the people rushing to get home before curfew began and you would notice armed men with automatic weapons in uniforms to ensure now one was in the streets. Martial law was imposed by the dictator Ferdinand Marcos and even speaking his name was only done in

92

hushed tones. The villages in the PI as we called it, were very poor and the children reminded me of the Campo.

Children of the Philippines

There were times when I was called upon to do shore duty in Olongapo. I remember one dark and rainy night me and my shipmate Robert, a Latino Marine from East Los Angeles, went out and patrolled the streets and went inside the bars and we heard this large boom hit outside the bar. We ran outside and laughed as we saw this guy get himself up from the muddy and sandy street, wipe his pants and the mud from his face, and said to us; Don't worry the ground stopped my fall. Time for a San Miguel." Going into town and back to the gate we had to walk across a bridge where natives would be in small pongas (carved out wooden boats holding 3 people) with small netted baskets and swimming in the murkey water below. Outside of Olongapo were hills and villages where many of the natives lived and carved out their existence.

Small Village in the Philippines

VIETNAM AND IDI AMIN

At the end of each rest and relaxation in our port of call in the Philippines we would complete our maintenance on our computers, bring onboard tons of fresh and frozen food, and watch the Air Group complete their work on the planes that needed attention. Then off to sea we went with our main station being the South China Sea and Vietnam. The Paris Peace Accords (17) were initially signed in 1973 and was broadcast to the country as Peace with Honor by Richard Nixon. Even though a ceasefire was agreed to early in 1973, resulting in a Nobel Peace prize by Henry Kissinger, by forces in Vietnam and the United States the war continued thru 1975 even as the United States started to withdraw forces. The USS Enterprise was the lead ship as part of US Task Force 77 in the seventh fleet and I spent over 70% of my time at sea as we were continually deployed.

Vietnam was at war since 1955 starting with the French and the US getting directly involved in 1965 and ended over 20 years later in 1975. From 1964 to 1975 it is estimated that there were approximately 1.3 million casualties including the death of 57,000 American soldiers. The cost of war continued to be unbearable for the US economy and in 1968 alone the US spent over 77 Billion dollars on the war. In the beginning, as the politicians talked about stopping communism, the country supported the war but later as the war dragged on and we continued to see our soldiers being killed and shown the violence and blood in our living rooms the anti-war movement rose across the country. Even on my ship we would discussions about the war, but regardless our duty was to do our jobs, ensure our planes got in the air and support our role. On a clear day in the South China sea on the 29th of April in 1975 I felt a violent shutter of our aircraft carrier and I was shocked as our ship's nuclear reactors were fully engaged to turn our 8 massive propellers at full power as we made a tight turn and leaned toward the water. As we made that turn we must have been going over 40-45 knots, about 50 miles an hour.

The ship itself was powered by 4 nuclear reactors and it was 80 feet from the deck to the waterline, so it was a huge ship and it moved effortlessly through the oceans. It was constructed with 60,000 tons of steel and over 230 miles of piping and underneath the flight deck was the hanger bay with over 5 acres. We had been conducting round the clock air operations as the US continued to monitor the movement of the North Vietnamese. I remembered seeing the Fleet Admiral come aboard and walking alongside my captain on the flight deck for a meeting the day before our ship changed direction dramatically. We were not told immediately what our new orders were, but we found out soon enough. We were part of Operation Frequent Wind (18) and our mission was to rescue the last Americans in Saigon and the Embassy. We sent helicopters to help transport the fleeing citizens of

South Vietnam and used the rooftop of the embassy for the last of those who would flee. We evacuated over 100,000 in Vietnam and Cambodia as part of our mission. The North Vietnamese Army had broken the terms of the Paris Peace Accords and were brutalizing the South Vietnamese as they took over the country. The US had sent a Marine detachment to Thailand in February to prepare for the evacuation of Phnom Penh, Cambodia as the brutality of war was being rained on their airport and the outskirts of the city.

The United States was still recovering from the wake of Watergate and Congress did not support the South Vietnamese with promised financial aid, weapons, and military support as outlined in the peace plan. This emboldened the North Vietnamese to gain strength and conquer the South. We had sent a small group of Marines to the Tan Son Nhat Airport outside the city of Saigon to protect this strategic part of the city and begin evacuating at-risk South Vietnamese citizens, but the forces were under-manned, and the Viet Cong were quickly winning the battle. We did successfully evacuate over 50,000 South Vietnamese from the airport, but we had to abandon it due to the enemy overtaking it. I had heard that our President, Gerald Ford considered providing more aid to the South Vietnamese as they did not have the weapons or the men to defend their capital and our Marine detachment onboard was on alert status. However due to political pressure and the weariness of the American people about the involvement of the U.S. he decided to let the South Vietnamese defend themselves.

Many of the locals would leave with only the clothes on their backs and take their families into old boats and they begin going down the rivers out to the sea, knowing that our task force was supporting operations to help their country. In some cases, a lot of the South Vietnamese citizens who helped the Americans during the conflict were hanging over the sides of their boats as they tried to get away and have the Americans save them. Lots of the locals were put onto helicopters to safety and some of the old helicopters were shoved overboard to the Vietnam Seas. Many of these Vietnamese refugees, who totaled over 40,000 would ultimately be sent to Camp Pendleton on the California coast and later a great many of them would assimilate into our US culture and society. The total number of South Vietnamese evacuated in US Custody numbered over 138,000. Many became doctors, joined the military as enlisted men and officers, and others became teachers and merchants. Even though the United States and North Vietnam signed a peace treaty in 1973, war between the North and the South continued and ultimately ended in April 30, 1975 as the US evacuated from Vietnam and the North Vietnamese took over Saigon and renamed it Ho Chi Minh city. Charles McMahon and Darwin Lee Judge were the last two United States servicemen killed during the war and died on April 29, 1975 in a rocket attack one day before the Fall of Saigon.

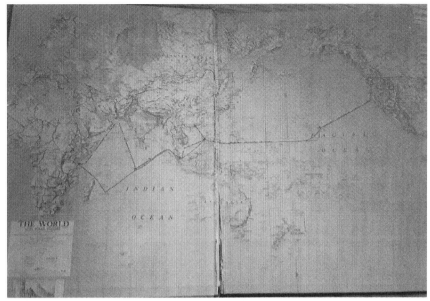

Deploynent:, see the world, if you can get off the ship.

The ships involved in the evacuations provided clothing and medical care to the people who had fled their native country. They were taken off the ships by all available transport to refugee camps in South East Asia. They were resettled in the United States, Canada, Australia and France among other countries. But they left their country and many of their families behind. We continued with our deployment on to Sumatra, and the Arabian sea. We had exercises with the Australian Navy and visited Hong Kong, Singapore and the Philippines and were called into the action as the Island of Mauritius was devasted by a typhoon and we rendered aid. We removed destroyed electrical poles, repaired their electrical infrastructure, provided food and water and sent medical officers to the island to tend to the children and the island people for needed aid. We returned to our homeport in Alameda in the fall of 1975. It was a blustery day and we had our ship lean as we crossed underneath the Golden Gate Bridge to be able to come into port. I could not help thinking that my dad went underneath this same bridge when he went to Korea over 20 years before and I wondered what he was thinking as he went to war. The shadow of his past crossed through my thoughts as I returned from Vietnam.

We deployed again in August of 1976. This was a challenging cruise as we were being shadowed by many submarines and long-range planes from the Soviet Union. We departed in September from Leyte Harbor in the Philippines for the transit to Australia for scheduled exercises with the New Zealand forces as well. In December we lost an F14 Tomcat (seen in the movie Top Gun) due to an engine failure before landing onboard due to a flight control malfunction. The tip of a wing clipped the tails of two planes parked on the port bow after the Tomcat struggled airborne. I saw both the pilot and his partner in the back eject high above the deck and splash down into the ocean below. The 1MC sounded the alarms and man overboard came on the speakers and you could hear it throughout the entire ship. Our S3A Helicopters and rescue personnel were quickly airborne and quickly moved to where our men were. Both were fished out of the ocean and were put into stokes stretchers and pulled into the helicopter and returned to our ship. A fire on the flight deck was contained and afterwards we surveyed the flight deck for FOD (Foreign Object Damage) to ensure there were no objects that could damage aircraft before resuming flight Ops. We were diverted to Africa off station in the seas out of Kenya, Africa as the dictator Idi Amin of the country of Uganda was threatening harm to our citizens. Idi Amin was known as the Butcher of Uganda and a brutal dictator and despot. International observers estimated that as many as 500,000 people were killed during his regime. As he realized the US Force that was being deployed, he relented and did not take anyone hostage. He decided not to execute on his published policies. As we returned to Alameda, California our massive ship went less than full power and leaned to go under the Golden Gate bridge at low tide and after the harbor was dredged.

From 1974 through 1979 I went on 3 nine-month deployments stopping in Hawaii, on the way to the Philippines. Then based on our objectives to Vietnam, Africa, Australia, Tasmania New Zealand,, Singapore and Hong Kong, In Hawaii I would always go visit the Pearl Harbor Memorial and in Singapore I could not believe how clean the streets were for an international city. We would have to adhere to all the customs and laws of each country we were in as we considered Ambassadors of the United States. Any misstep could land you in jail or possible a public flogging, as in Singapore. During our visit to Hong Kong me and one of guys I worked with, from Pasadena, went to the famed fishing village of Aberdeen. In Aberdeen in the 5th century a group of people emigrated to the southern outskirts of Hong Kong and lived their entire lives on their junk boats, fishing, trading and observing their ceremonies. The locals laughed at us when we started howling because we tried their Cantonese food and found it spicer than any salsa we ever had. Later in the afternoon we decided to go the outskirts as far away from the city as possible. We jumped in a cab and told him that we wanted to stay in a good in the mountains. He drove us through the streets and up through the mountain hills. As we arrived we noticed that there were only a few people speaking English and we made friends with this Irish guy. Turns out he was working the railroads and as we drank profusely that evening he opened up and said his money was destined for the Irish Republican Army for the cause. After turning in for the evening late we woke up late in the morning and hurried to get back to the ship. We did not make it. We had plan B. I asked the cabbie to take us to another place where we had set up communications. When we arrived there and identified ourselves we were reprimanded and then jumped in the last helicopters bound for our ship. I had a great time, but Captains Mast seemed like our future as missing ships movement is a serious offense. Luckily because we were getting a new captain they cancelled all Captains Mast.

. As I became proficient in my job I was promoted and was a pending First Class Petty Officer who managed the younger technicians as part of CIC support Group for our systems. I was confident, experienced and young. I enjoyed working with the various contractors as we tested out new operating systems before we went on deployment. While in port in Tasmania I happened to come across a search party on the cliffs overlooking a huge bluff. We found out they were searching for a little boy 3 and a little girl 2 who had unknowingly walked away from a group. Their parents were frantic and asked for our help. With luck I found the little boy and his little sister and was able to return them to their parents. We were invited to share tea, which was the term for dinner, with the family and accepted their offer and reciprocated by giving them a tour of our ship.

We had multiple Data Systems technicians who were specialists on Display Systems, Computer Systems, Navigation Systems, Payroll batch systems and our IOIC (Integrated Onboard Intelligence Center) Systems. I was determined to learn as many systems as I could, and I was awarded the Systems Designation as a result. I found out later that this designation was not given out without a lot of documentation and recommendations. During this deployment I took a closer look at a system called the KCMX and I asked who maintained it and what it was for. The person who had the previous expertise had just left the ship and no one really knew too much about it, so I begin to study its interfaces, what systems were connected to it and what systems it provided information to. What I found was that this was the heart of the system integrating data from Navigation, Radar Systems, Communications Systems and Fire Control Systems to our ACDS (Advanced Computer Decision Systems) platform. While others played cards, played their guitars, drank their coffee, and watched television, I poured through all the documentation and connected our diagnostic systems to become familiar with it.

Well, it was a good thing that I was curious. We were supposed to start flight Operations and prepare for our exercises with the Australia and New Zealand Navy and then suddenly all information on the Display Systems were frozen, our communications to our aircraft and other ships did not work and we needed to go to our emergency backups and the ACDS system screamed with multiple alerts. Everyone scrambled but I knew it had to be that KCMX that no one but me knew anything about. Well after conferring with our team and my Chief I started to diagnose what caused the problem. It seemed liked every 5 minutes our Officers from the Electronics department were coming up next to me asking me question after question; What's the problem, how will you fix it, how long will it take, how can you be sure. I had the machine opened up with probes connected to it and my schematics were spread on the tables around me and I could smell the odor of burnt circuits and I knew it was not going to be easy.

I had to bypass some integrated circuits with creative wiring, replaced damaged circuit boards, aligned the servos, and would run mini diagnostics as fast as I could. My Chief came up to me and asked me what he could do. I told him; "Chief, please. I really have to focus on this work, so keep all those officers away from me, I will give you an update every 30 minutes." I had another technician watching my every move trying to understand what I was doing. It was tense as our entire fleet was awaiting our ship, the USS Enterprise, which was designated as the Net Control Ship, as to when it would be ready. It took about 3 hours, and it felt like a lifetime, but I solved the problems. When we arrived back to our homeport in Alameda, 6 months later, I was quickly sent off the ship for formal training on that KCMX. My job was to get certification and teach it to someone else once I returned onboard. It's a good thing my Mom kept praying that I fix them because I surely did not do it on my own.

I spent over 6 ½ years in the US Navy with about 70% of time on the various oceans of the world and worked 12 hours on shift while at sea. I worked with young men from Kentucky, Nebraska, Ohio, California, New York, New Jersey, and we passed the time playing poker, running on the flight deck when there was no air operations underway, learning how to play guitar, telling stories of places we've been and places we were going to go. I would go up on deck in the Indian Ocean and look as far as I could see and the ocean seem to shimmer like a pane of glass, ever so smooth and quiet. We would watch as the blue flying fish would be attracted to our large wake and follow along side of us as at times as we cruised at low speed. I had friends who worked in the entertainment department which produced a daily television show of events around the world, of course they were censured, and of things that were happening onboard ship and a radio show as part of the Armed Forces Radio Network which ran 24 hours a day. I was asked to produce a radio show when I was off shift and it ran from 10 PM to 2 AM. I gladly accepted and played the Blues, Rock n Rock, and R&B and took requests and did interviews. I played some Chicano music too with the likes of Ray Barretto, Santana and Joe Bataan.

I got out of the Navy as my last stop was the Bremerton Shipyards in the state of Washington for drydock overhaul in my last 7 months. During the years on my ship I would see other Latinos who were boatswains' mates, cooks, and also some medics. But the majority worked in supply handling all the different containers that our ship needed to get through our cruises. I was able to get a shore warehouse assignment and I joined the NAVY softball team. Our team was comprised mostly of these supply guys who were always seemed to be in shape, strong and athletic. We traveled for the Navy, first in the state of Washington then later to California and played a lot of other military units and a lot of civilians for practice. We were undefeated for a long time. I remember we would play sometimes 6 games a week. Mostly because we were young, and a lot of these guys were totally in shape after working on handling supplies day in and day out. On this softball I felt at home as 80% of the players were Latinos from California, Chicago and New York. We spoke Spanish as we enjoyed competing and for 6 months I felt like I was back home. I played 3rd base on my team and made a lot of friends for that moment in time. One of guys actually had tried out for the Yankees and was set to go to the minors until he threw out his arm. Another guy was so fast, he was a left-handed batter that he would hit it on the ground on purpose to the shortstop and he would beat the throw to first base. Well we needed to win our last 2 games to make the Interservice Sectionals. If we won, then it would be on to Nationals and I would have to think about re-enlisting to keep playing. Well we lost, so no worries.

I had signed on as a 17-year-old to be part of the military and at the age of 24 I was going to end my time. It was a time of maturation, of being a young adult, of having responsibilities to others. I felt the challenge of serving your country and continuing to grow up a half a world away from my family and friends. I learned so much from so many and I did see the world. I considered re-enlisting if I was offered the Monterey Weather Station where they had the most advanced computers at that time. Well I did not get that one. I was still torqued at the NAVY as I was recommended for NESEP, Naval Enlisted Scientific Education Program. The Navy would have paid for me to go to college and I would come out as an officer. But it never happened as the Navy pulled back the funds to support it. Leaving the service was a big decision, however like some of my shipmates said, "Being in the service is like being in a mental hospital, some people get cured and some people never get out." The Navy tried to keep me and offered a Bonus to stay, but after they did not offer me the opportunity to work on the newest computers at the Naval Postgraduate School in Monterey, I decided not to re-enlist.

When I entered the service I was a Chicano, arrogant and angry, but retuned as a young man who would soon be home in Pittsburg with confidence and be with my family and the abrazos that I had missed as I went to Vietnam, different countries, and the Oceans of the World. As I was leaving he service, after all those years, it was a whole new world for me that I was rejoining. It was now almost 1980 and my friends, those who rose above the poverty and the drugs, were now in construction, educators, civil engineers, programmers and part of Corporate America. In the oceans of the world there was no room for racism or discrimination to get in the way of opportunity and responsibility. In that world it was RHIP, Rank Has Its Privileges. I had replaced my arrogance with pride that I earned as I matured, a Chicano from the neighborhood, who became a leader on one of the mightiest ships in the world. I was Captain Kirk.

LAWRENCE LIVERMORE NATIONAL LABORATORY

The commercial computer field was starting to explode in 1979. I had been trained as a Data Systems specialist on different computer systems, programming and understanding how to isolate problems and provide solutions. In 1979 the IBM PC was two years from being developed and available to the public. In 1979 IBM, General Electric, Hewlett Packard, Sperry Univac, Measurex and Control Data Corporation were providing the systems, programs and expertise to high end manufacturing, research, and stores likes Montgomery Ward, Sears and Roebuck and others. Fast systems that needed to manage huge amounts of data and perform different business functions. I had just joined the Navy when the birth of the networking in 1973 began as a predecessor to the internet. In 1979 the IBM PC was still two years away with many people buying computer kits as hobby enthusiasts. After I submitted my resume to 26 companies, I received positive feedback from 21 of them. I was flown to Minneapolis to interview with Sperry Rand Corporation and was also offered a job at Ford Aerospace to manage their commercial systems at the Roosevelt Roads facility in Puerto Rico. But I wanted to stay close to home and went to multiple interviews with the Lawrence Livermore National Laboratory. I had to go through a final interview with the FBI in San Francisco as the work, if offered, would be considered above top secret working for the Department of Energy. The interview by the FBI felt like an interrogation not an interview, but I was honest and after the FBI shared that they done a deep background check on my life I left that office wondering what was going to happen next.

I was offered a position and accepted a position as a senior technical specialist at the Lab with the Computer Engineering Group. Little did I know that it would be the greatest professional experience in my life.

The Lawrence Livermore Lab is located about 50 miles east of San Francisco in the Livermore valley next to farmland and wineries outside the town of Livermore. Livermore lies below the hills of the Altamont Pass, infamous because of the multiple deaths during a Rolling Stones concert in 1969. Other bands played including Santana, Jefferson Airplane, and Crosby Stills Nash and Young. The Grateful Dead refused to perform due to the violence. It was estimated that 300,000 attended as it was a free festival and documented in the movie Give Me Shelter. Across the street from the Lab was the Sandia Industries Corporation. That was the company that used the research and testing completed at the Lab and used it in their manufacturing for nuclear weapons. In the early days the Livermore Radiation Laboratory, as it was called, was created as competition to the Los Alamos Laboratory, where the first nuclear bomb was created as part of the Manhattan project during world war two. The goal was to advance thermonuclear weapons research, and this was the basis for funding, deemed to be necessary because the Russians had produced their first nuclear device some five years earlier than our pundits had predicted. Edward Teller (31), the father of the Hydrogen bomb, lobbied and proposed that the lab be created driven by the Atomic Energy Commission with it run by the University of California and was founded in 1952.

In the beginning it became apparent that the use of computers was needed to support research, and a staff was created by John von Neumann (Who many consider the father of the original core computing design), and he was able to secure the first computer to aid his case, the UNIVAC. Sid Fernback was appointed head of the Computer department at the laboratory in 1952. John Von Neumann was the guy who really described the first computer architecture model, Of course in those days of 1952 there was no computer department, there were no computer programming papers, and the position of Computer Scientist had not been created by anyone or anyplace. In those days It was not even considered a profession, such was the ground that was being advanced. There was no history, no books, everything had to be created. Innovation became the thriving forces for advancement of and use of computers in high performance computational calculations. Sid, an early student of J. Robert Oppenheimer, who was the project manager for the Los Alamos Laboratory and developed the atom bomb, at UC Berkeley went about using that UNIVAC to begin aiding nuclear research. Dr. Oppenheimer 's Top Secret clearance was later revoked due to blacklisting and politics. The Univac computer was used by CBS to predict the result of the 1952 election and had to be transported from Philadelphia and reassembled. In those days early computers were huge as even 10,000 words of memory would need to be housed in a cabinet 8 feet tall and 16 feet long.

The Univac computer still was not fast enough for the Lab and consequently they then bought the next computers from IBM. The computers from IBM also could not deliver the performance required by the physicists and scientists and the laboratory started to create specifications for a machine that could handle the jobs they ran and awarded the contract to Sperry Rand. This first one was called the Livermore Advanced Research Computer (LARC). They would assign a mathematician with a physicist to program and review the results. Those were the earliest systems, with discrete circuits, transistors, huge core memories. Speed was driven by design. Through the years beyond UNIVAC, the laboratory began buying, programming and integrating systems made by IBM, Control Data Corporation (CDC), and Cray Research (1978) and used the first designed super computers. In the early days computational programming and competition was tolerated and encouraged. Computational speed was paramount for research and the main computer center housed the computers, tape drives, disk drives and peripherals for these batch intensive jobs. Because of the requirements of the lab the OCTOPUS environment networking all these systems together was designed and later the first high-performance Time-Sharing System was designed. Eventually The laboratory created a second computational facility called the Magnetic Fusion Energy Research Laboratory and it considered the best in the world.

The Livermore campus, in 1979 was about 1 Mile Square in size, with approximately 6,200 people working there. I was assigned to the Computer Engineering Group and the people that I worked with were beyond ultra-smart. It seemed like half the staff had a PhD or more with names like Edward Teller; father of the Hydrogen Bomb, George Michel; leader of Super Computing and founder of the International Supercomputer Conference, Harold Brown a nuclear physicist who later became Secretary of Defense under Jimmy Carter. The staff was diverse with the top minds from all over the US, and countries like Germany, China and Persia. The buildings that housed the research and the scientists and engineers were compartmentalized (segregated) throughout the campus with sectors divided by different levels of security from Confidential, to Secret, to Top Secret. Because of the team I worked with, I was assigned a Q clearance by the department of Energy, which meant I could work, as appropriate on Top Secret programs. There were bicycles all over the campus. If you had to go across campus you would just use it to go from place to place when the weather was good. If there was a problem with the bicycle, you just set-it upside down and there were people who canvassed the campus, picked them up, and repaired them and put them back in service. When it rained you could call 2-TAXI give them your starting location, destination and badge number and they would identify a route that took you thru the various security checkpoints.

Beyond Nuclear research the computation group expanded into other others, Magnetic Fusion, Laser Fusion, Unix Operating Systems, Compilers, Mass storage devices, Laser isotopes (used for surgeries today), voice recognition, baseband, broadband, research to increase agricultural crop yields. You name it was done. The Computational staff designed an integrated network to link us the campus and other facilities in the US such as MIT, NSA, Fermi lab in Chicago among others. When the manufacturers wanted to have their new systems tested the Laboratory acted as a "BETA" site for affirmations of their designs. And at times the physicists and mathematicians would design all these incredible programs and find underlying design flaws that impacted speed and accuracy, much to the chagrin of the original manufacturers. So, beyond the first CDC, IBM and CRAY big box supercomputers the early Digital Equipment Corporation (DEC), SUN and other manufacturer computers were tested out and improved upon.

Because of my clearance I was invited to all the high-powered sessions that many scientists would have. I went to a few and realized that the conversation was in a language that I had no understanding of. It would take about 5 minutes into the session and I would realize that I was in a room of total genius's and who did nothing but think, engage in hyper conversations, challenged existing scientific laws and created new discoveries. I would attend engineering sessions with the department that I was assigned and they filled me with further education on design, analytics, broadband, baseband, performance and distributed computing principles, I was assigned to work with a systems development team in support of multiple teams of scientists located through-out the lab complex as part of a remote job entry network, the father of a distributed network. These teams would work on such things as advanced voice recognition, high energy explosives, laser isotope separation, laser fusion, and many other complex programs and projects. I was responsible to 60 teams of chemical engineers, scientists and physicists to ensure the computer systems they used were always accessible and performed as expected and integrated to the main computer centers. I was immediately provided with the tools manage these systems and supporting them across the range of the laboratory including the Nevada Test Site.

The Nevada Test Site located in the Nevada desert of Tonopath was the facility used for underground Nuclear Bomb testing. I was assigned to manage the computing and communications systems for the Nevada Test Site. I took specialized training to understand how to work on Time Division Multiplexors, their interfaces and frequently worked with personnel assigned by AT&T, EG&G and the General Services Administration. When the communications links would fail in Livermore, I would be asked to come into those rooms, which were classified higher than Top Secret, and they would sanitize them by clearing out any agency communication papers and cover the equipment that I would not be working on before I was allowed in. On a monthly basis I was flown to Nevada, usually on a Laboratory plane, into a private and secured airfield outside located approximately 140 miles North West from Las Vegas to Tonopath. I would then go through a security debrief and be directed to take a car to the test range, is located 30 miles southeast. It is located northwest of Area 51 and is on the northern part the Nellis Range. Area 51 is the super-secret facility managed by the government and military that supposedly captured an alien flying saucer in the 1950s. The test range is restricted as it is used for nuclear weapons research, stockpile testing, and testing of nuclear weapons delivery systems. At times I would see experimental and classified aircraft flying low in the desert as I headed for my debriefing station. Once I arrived on station, I was escorted into the underground facility where the scientists, Nuclear Regulatory Agency staff and engineers were conducting their work. In those days the US would perform Nuclear blasts underground and my job was to ensure that all the computing and communication systems were validated before every test, which occurred monthly. The results of the test would immediately be sent to Livermore, other National Laboratories and Agencies.

I also had the opportunity to be assigned to a development project for the Advanced Research Projects Agency (ARPA) setting up the facility for a VAX-MP (4) cluster that was being developed to support some work with the Berkeley laboratory. The VAX cluster was a special designed computer system by the Digital Equipment Corporation, and we used it as Unix based environment and as I received the ARPA equipment, we prepared to integrate all the systems together. Another high visibility project was the development of the micro-multiplexor systems that were used to integrate the various labs that there in use by the scientists and increase the amount of jobs they could perform. I was assigned to de-bug and isolate failures for these systems and make repairs before we installed them through-out the lab complex. Our team built and delivered a system for the Oak Ridge National Laboratory, located in Tennessee, to support their research. Later we competed to see if we could setup a micro-multiplexor which was sent to Seymour Cray to his Chippewa Falls facility.

LLNL was an exciting environment to be part of because of the world class people you were a part of, and the projects and technologies that were being developed. The Lab would allow 2 hours at lunch, one hour for health and one hour for lunch daily. A lot of us would take daily runs along the California Aqueduct and we would see some bikers who would eventually make the Olympics. What the Lab found out is that they needed everyone to stay healthy. People would take less time off for sick leave and this would also lesson their stress and improve productivity.

In the beginning I lived in a 1-bedroom care-takers home on a pig farm about 2 miles away from the Laboratory in between the Concannon and the Wente wineries. Even when I wanted to walk to work these scientists would pull over and push all their books away and have me get in to get to work. I joined the LLNL Bowling league and even outside of work I found out that all these people were super competitive. I was assigned to initially work in the "cooler" a section of the laboratory that was set apart for those who had not yet gained their final clearance. We were giving assignments and training so that we could become indoctrinated in the methods of the programs to which we were to be assigned. In the morning of January 24 at 11 AM as I was in a discussion a design with a senior scientist the stool that I was sitting on began to vibrate violently and knocked me off of it. I looked at the ceilings and I could see the neon light fixtures shaking back and forth. It was an earthquake with a magnitude of 5.5 and as it continued we evacuated and as the bright sun hit our eyes we could clearly see the 50-foot electrical poles flexing back and forth. The alarm in the laboratory went off and later we found that it was caused as a monitor measured a trace amount of highly radioactive tritium that began to leak. The horn sounded about 45 minutes later and we were given the all clear to return to our stations. The aftershocks would continue in the following weeks as well as another strong earthquake 2 days later. I could feel the aftershocks at night and in the early morning as I slept on the floor of my studio on the pig-farm.

The town of Livermore was about 55 miles East of San Francisco and it was a small town back then. Outside of the town next to the rolling hills were old style pig and sheep farms which had been around since the turn of the century. If you weren't at the Lab or in town you most likely would be traveling East to the hills on Site 300 about 15 miles away from the Lab where we did a lot of explosives testing. A lot of us who worked as the lab, and who were casually called Lab Rats by the people in town, would go the Livermore Saloon after a long day's work. Outside the saloon there usually would be about 8-10 dressed Harley Motorcycles with their owners inside the saloon. Many of us parked across the street in an empty lot and raced across the street to make it to the saloon. Picture all these physicists (with thick coke bottle lenses framed by their black glasses) with their computer printouts spread out on their tables, with bikers playing pool at the end of the saloon enjoying the music on the jukebox playing loud hits of the Grateful Dead, Deep Purple and other rock bands. The farmers would be standing next to the bar or on stools as they drank huge glasses of beer with their overalls muddy from a full day of work at the fields. The beer was cold, and the food was bad but at times the local pizza places would deliver pizza and everyone would yell that it was for them, and it was shared with the ones who were the quickest to get at it.

I enjoyed returning to California after my time in the military and being with my Mom and my family. But when I visited Pittsburg I could see a transformation that was happening. The Centro where I spent much of my youth with other young Chicanos was now gone, the Latino political officials also seemed a part of the past as well and the stores in downtown Pittsburg kept disappearing. The UFW gains and contracts that were signed in the 70s were disappearing and the farmworkers which led to the membership of the UFW to shrink in the early 80s and organizing the workers was slowing to a trickle. The activism of my youth and the excitement of being part of change now seemed far behind me and I started to focus on my career. I was not alone. Ethnic studies were still being taught in many schools and colleges but over time these education programs would begin to start disappearing as funding was being cut little by little, year by year and the progressive attitudes and leaders of the Chicano movement seemed to fade away.

Our Pittsburg family, getting ready to share a meal.
LtoR: Mom, Grace, Erma, Me, Irene

I spent almost 5 years working at the Lawrence Livermore Laboratory, from 1979 through 1984, and learned more than I could have ever expected from so many creative and futurist scientists and physicists. What I remember most was the leadership that was exhibited on a daily basis, the expectation to perform at the highest level, and the help that would immediately be available to support anyone when needed. There were people from all races and ethnic races working at the Laboratory, but again upon reflecting I noticed that there was a real lack of Latinos working as Engineers, Computer Scientists and Chemists. I do not believe it was by design but by the lack of Latinos in the sciences during those times. Latinos are descendants of the Mayans who were gifted mathematicians, astronomers, and detailed that a solar year was slightly more than 365 days. There were some that were acclaimed, including Severo Ochoa an award-winning Biochemist who won the Nobel Prize in 1959 and Luis Alvarez who won the Physics Nobel prize in 1968. But for most of Latinos examples of achievement in the sciences was mostly unknown. That is our heritage however somehow that history did not seem to resonate with Latinos in the United States, in our families, in the school systems, and in most sectors of the economy. In the laboratory discrimination was not tolerated as everyone who worked there was considered the best that the country had to offer and there was no room for ideologies and beliefs that did not contribute to the mission of success and wellness.

The LLNL contributed many advancements in technology, science, biology, chemistry, precision manufacturing and other fields. In March of 1979 the experimental project Atmospheric Radioactive Advisory Center was called into emergency service to track the path of the radiation during the Three Mile Island Reactor Accident. The center has responded to hundreds of alerts and incidents since operations began. Key events include the 1980 Titan II missile explosion in Damascus, Arkansas; the Chernobyl nuclear power plant meltdown in 1986; the Kuwaiti oil fires during and after the Persian Gulf War in 1991; the 1991 Mount Pinatubo eruption; an industrial cesium-137 release in Algeciras, Spain, in 1998; and the Fukushima disaster in 2011 in Japan. The laboratory mission has changed over the years with a big focus on technology transfer to meet the challenges of industry. An example is the automotive industry. The automotive industry has used the LLNL LS-DYNA to make great leaps in safety research with multi-dimensional crash simulations with more than 1.5 million points.

LLNL researchers reconfigured one arm of the Nova laser to achieve a highly significant advance in laser technology: a petawatt laser. In 1996, the petawatt laser set a power record of 1.25 quadrillion (a million billion) watts—more than 1,200 times the U.S. power generating capacity— for a duration less than a trillionth of a second. The laser's ultrashort pulses and extremely high irradiance opened up entirely new physical regimes to study. Experiments have split atoms, created antimatter, and generated a well-focused, intense proton beam—all firsts for a laser. In 2016, the Laboratory set new records with the High-Repetition Rate Advanced Petawatt Laser (HAPLS) system, which is designed to generate 10 pulses per second, each 30 quadrillionths of second long with greater than one petawatt peak power. The system includes many breakthrough technologies, including the use of laser diodes as flashlamps, which reduces system size and power requirements. HAPLS has been delivered to the Extreme Light Infrastructure (ELI) Beamlines facility in the Czech Republic, where it will provide experimenters with unique opportunities to advance their understanding of the fundamental nature of energy and matter.

The 5 years that I worked as a part of the LLNL environment, with top engineers and scientists and its innovative atmosphere and emerging technologies enriched my knowledge in ways I could not imagine. The LLNL culture of diversity and inclusion, allowed me to stretch the limits of my curiosity, skills and accelerated my ability to quickly learn, adapt and provided me with the foundation for leadership.

GO EAST YOUNG MAN

After returning from the service, living in the Bay Area for almost 5 years, I was yearning for a new experience. In the fall of 1984, and after almost 5 years at Lawrence Livermore National Laboratory (LLNL) I left to join Sperry Univac Computer Corporation and took an assignment as a field engineer to work on the Land Based Engineering Facility (LBEF) supporting submarines in their Newport Rhode Island Facility. Newport Rhode Island was south of Boston on the East Coast and I wanted to get to know the North East coast of the United States. I had been working at LLNL as part of the Computations Group supporting the many physicists and scientists doing research on Nuclear design, Magnetic Fusion, High Performance Computing and many other exciting R&D projects. Many of these physicists and scientists attended my going away roast. My colleagues were surprised that I would even consider leaving as the Lawrence Livermore National Laboratory, one of 6 in the United States, was considered prestigious. I packed my car with all my belongings and left California with no maps for guidance and headed East. My plan was to go across country and once I hit the Ocean on the Eastern seaboard, I would go North to Rhode Island.

As I went across country, I saw how huge it really was and marveled at how the Geography changed in front of me and all the small towns littered across the country. I went south via highway 99 in California then East across Mojave Desert to the mountains of Flagstaff in Arizona and through to New Mexico. While crossing New Mexico I could see why they started the Atomic Bomb Manhattan project as it seemed like all I saw was the color red in the desert and plains and it was so hot you could see adobe houses everywhere. When I was in Oklahoma I veered north to Kansas and felt like I was enveloped by corn fields of Kansas. I remember getting gas in an oasis in Kansas in this real small town and an attractive young woman wearing shorts due to the heat of the day asking me where I was going. "Mister, where you headed? I'm starting a new life and a new job in Newport Rhode Island and I don't know anyone there." She was filling my car with gas and then said; "I've been here all my life and I ain't been nowhere. I guess I'll die here too, wish I was going with you." I should have said get in, but I didn't. I left Kansas and kept rolling across the country and veered through the mountains of Kentucky and to the coast in Virginia. Then North as I went onward to Rhode Island.

Newport itself was on the southern part of Aquidneck Island, with the Island located 20 miles south of Massachusetts, with the town of Middletown about 5 miles North with farmland in the middle and the northern part of the island being industrial and where the Land Based Engineering Facility (LBEF) location was located. Newport was a beautiful place with history;

John F Kennedy was married there, beautiful yacht harbor, mansions and jazz clubs. I lived initially in a 2 room older home in Middletown and would travel up the winding road to LBEF. We would work rotating shifts and regardless of which shift we had after work we would visit the local bars in Middletown, enjoy our lobster bisque, beers all around and we had a saying; "If you're going to hang around you got to buy a round." Nobody in Middletown or Newport knew about Cesar Chavez as the Chicano movement might as well been on the moon. This was the land of the Pilgrims and if your family did not come over in the Mayflower you weren't local. There was however a small Portuguese community and I tried to understand their language, but it was different enough from Spanish that I didn't understand it. When they talked they seemed to slur every other word as they spoke to each other. They were a proud people and would tell me that the Portuguese were the best sailors and navigators in world in the 15th century and that they mapped Africa, Asia and Brazil. After about 3 months in Newport learning how to test, diagnose and maintain different computing systems I was reassigned to work in Minnesota to help support development of the next generation fault tolerant computers as part of a multi-million contract. I would be 1 of 5 Field Engineers from across the country that Sperry selected to gain the expertise to become experts for these systems as they were delivered to their customers.

I arrived in Minneapolis in late in September of 1984 before the snows decided they wanted to make their home there. Newport and Middletown seemed as small as Pittsburg and Brentwood, but Minneapolis was the big city. Again, I did not know one person as I arrived in what seemed like a world of Scandinavians and not knowing what to expect. When It would snow the reflections from the snow would be so bright you would not be able to see 1 foot in front of you or in any direction. Minnesota was also the coldest place I thought could ever exist. In the cold of the winter you would have to have your engine block connected with a cord to an electrical outlet to keep it warm enough to start your engine. I quickly found out that the kid from California did not know how to drive in the snow. I had a Mazda RX7 sports car and when the first snows came down after work, I drove my car and that's when I hit the black ice. I hit my brakes and my car did a 360-degree spin on an empty stretch of road as I was getting to a stop sign. If that was not enough the next day the snows really started to come down and when I was going to my apartment my cars wheels spun as I went into a full snow embankment. Luckily Karma was on my side because 3 guys came, like manna from heaven, came out of the apartments and dug me out.

I told the guys at work what happened and gave me a hard time, but they decided they would pick me up and drive me to work and back. That winter I learned how to play broomball and enjoy the game of Ice Hockey as my roommate had friends on the Minnesota University team who were ranked number 1. It was a cold winter I thought, but these folks in Minnesota did not seem to mind and they went about their business outside and did not let the snow make their lives miserable. It was 6 degrees in January and 9 degrees in February, but I learned what windchill was all about. When the winds would blow the temperature would feel 20 or 30 degrees colder when it hit your skin, so you had better have the right clothes on and always, always, have sometime on your head. Well the springtime came, and I saw people come alive and as it got warm by early June the pool started to come alive at my apartment. I learned how to play tennis and competed against my two roommates about 3 hours a day after work on Monday thru Sunday. I also and lost a lot of golf balls as I was introduced to the great game of golf.

I spent a year in Minnesota with the development teams completed their testing and initial manufacturing of the next generation computers that would be put in service for multiple Universities, Government run organizations and the military. These were the first fault tolerant computers with proprietary micro integrated circuits that the military asked Sperry to develop. In 1985 I would be asked to represent the company and go to General Electric, Johns Hopkins University and IBM initially to begin installation, testing, and training. The world of Computers had changed, and people were playing games with Nintendo, the TCP/IP protocol was established for linking different type computers, Michael Dell started his computer and started selling cheaper priced personal computer clones and people rushed to buy them. The computers that I worked on were high performance and had specialized programs that were developed by hundreds of programmers for supporting big business and also by the department of defense. Working in Minnesota I would be 1 of 5 Field Engineers in the world that had the familiarity, the training, and expertise to do this work.

I had two roommates in Minnesota, and in November I was asked by my roommate Allan if I would go to Lansing Michigan, which was close to Minnesota for Thanksgiving with his family. A bonus was that we were asked to house-sit next door to his parents. Allan's family was all American with his Mom making the dinner and the pies and his dad, who I called Mr. T, a big man who was no-nonsense and worked in the American car industry. His dad had just returned from Russia where he was investigating how the company that made the huge steel rims for the big earth movers that worked in the rugged mountains. He was able to tell me the stories of how the rims would be crushed when they overloaded their containers because they would pour vodka into their bellies because it was too cold. Well it was the day before Thanksgiving, Nov 23 and Allan and I were watching this great college game between Boston College and University of Miami.

Miami was heavily favored but the Boston College Eagles had a kid named Doug Flutie. Well the game went back and forth, and Miami took the lead with just a few seconds left. Well dinner was ready, and his parents kept calling us for dinner. They said, "The game is over, what can happen in 10 seconds." So, we turned off the TV and walked across the yard to their house. It is now regarded as the Miracle in Miami, or the Hail Flutie game, and the most memorable in sports as Doug Flutie threw a last ditch desperation pass 63 yards and it was caught in the end zone with no time left; CAUGHT BY BOSTON COLLEGE, I DON'T BELIEVE IT! IT'S A TOUCHDOWN. When we walked into the house for dinner, they still had it on, and we missed it. Boston College won 47-45. I would finally see Doug Flutie play 14 years later in 1998 when I lived in Buffalo and he was a starter for the Buffalo Bills.

After my 3-month temporary assignment turned into a 1-year experience in Minnesota, I returned to Aquidneck Island in Rhode Island and begin working again at the LBEF facility as the new fault-tolerant systems were delivered. I installed them and trained my friends on how they were designed and how to isolate failures. While in Minnesota working for Sperry I met 1 other Latino who was from the state of Colorado. Colorado has always had a high population of Latinos, however he told me as a group they considered themselves derived from Spaniards and did not embrace the Chicano name or the struggles that were prevalent in California or Chicago. That was a revelation for me at that, but he was smart, and I respected his perspective. When I returned to Newport I found a room in a Victorian house in the downtown of Newport where I lived for 6 months. I moved in with my friend Joseph Albicocco who I worked with at the lab. Joseph lived in a caretaker's home adjoining the graves and headstones located in an old cemetery that was established in 1640. He told me the story of when his father was young in Sicily living by Palermo as a carpenter when he made the decision to move to the United States and he sent Joe's mother and older sister ahead to Ellis Island with the wooden suitcase he had made for them.

He joined them once he saved up enough money and they moved to Ansonia, Connecticut. Joe had just traded his Harley Davidson motorcycle and was rebuilding a red 1956 Porsche, which he always seemed to be working on. Joe was a great Italian cook, and our friends would always stop by to savor his new creations. One evening Joe took part of his engine over the Newport bridge to Cranston so that they could do specialized work on it. It was about 11 PM when he returned, and I asked him the name of the place where he took his engine part. His eyes grew wide as he started naming the place and then he saw the fire that was engulfing that business on our television. Luckily the building where he left it was not the one on fire, and once we found out we opened a bottle of wine to celebrate his near misfortune. Newport was an exciting town with lots to do and lots to see and I used to walk to the comedy clubs, have drinks at the local jazz clubs, and enjoy fresh seafood at the restaurants on the wharf. I would drive along the scenic coast of Newport and stop off at Cliff Walk and enjoy the views of the ocean and drive along Mansion row see these huge buildings created by the Vanderbilt family and the Breakers mansions, and stroll into the International Tennis Hall of Fame.

In Newport I visited St. Mary's Church which was where John F Kennedy and Jacqueline Bouvier were married. I would walk upon the grounds of the Island Cemetery where many prominent Americans were buried including; Oliver Hazard Perry-Naval Hero in the War of 1812, Major General Sherman- Hero of the Civil War, and others. The citizens of Newport were devastated as Americas Cup schooner sailing race was lost in 1983 to a team from Australia. The American team was skippered by Dennis Conner and it was the first loss in 132 years. Americas Cup has never been hosted in Newport Rhode Island since that loss.

SAN DIEGO

After working almost 3 years on the East Coast, with my sojourn to Minnesota, I was longing to come back to California and I asked my boss for a transfer and of course the answer was no. I was missing my Mom, my family, my friends and my culture. I was deemed too critical to their program on the newest computers that our company Sperry was about to manufacture and deliver to the US military. Karma came knocking on my door. A friend of mine who I had worked with on the USS Enterprise was in Los Angeles and he contacted me and asked if I would take an assignment for Hughes Aircraft Company, a division of General Motors, working in San Diego. My friend, Michael Burns, and I used to shadow box in the gym onboard ship as he was an accomplished lightweight boxer. Michael schooled me in every time he had me in the gym, but regardless the workout was great. Before joining the Navy as an amateur he had fought the Puerto Rican fighter Wilfred Benitez and I asked him what he thought; "He was lightning fast, and I couldn't catch him". Wilfred eventually became a professional boxer and lost his title to Sugar Ray Leonard. After Michael got out of the Navy he fought under a different name in San Diego before his wife found out, and that was the end. Couldn't catch Wilfred Benitez and couldn't fool his wife.

After Sperry found out I had an offer from their competition they did everything they could to convince me to stay with them including approving my transfer to California working in research in the city of Malibu. They offered per diem at a rate of an extra $1,200 a month tax free, which was a lot in 1987, If I would take the position. But I had given my word to my friend Michael and I packed my car with everything I owned, and I did not own that much, and off I went back West across country to Los Angeles where Hughes Aircraft was located before moving down to San Diego. This time I took the northern route across country through Pennsylvania, across the rolling plains of Iowa, Captain Kirk was from Iowa, across the country I went on the Northern route and to the south of Oregon. I made sure I went through the redwood forest as I went south to California. As I got to California I went down Highway 1 and enjoyed the Pacific coastline and the small towns on my way to Los Angeles. I stopped in Pittsburg to visit my Mom and surprised her as I came into to town and told her about my new job. After 3 days of hugs, food, music and family I continued my trip.

I stayed in Los Angeles for 3 months working with different departments until I was ready to go to San Diego. After approval by the government I was assigned to the Computer Design Engineering Systems (CDES) in the Point Loma area of San Diego next to the Pacific Ocean. The facility I was assigned to was responsible for the upgrading of the existing Naval Tactical Data

Systems with the new generation fault tolerant computers and their operating systems and applications programs with updated engineering systems. Additionally, they were tasked to begin the design of the AI (artificial intelligence) systems using commercial systems that would eventually evolve into replacing the sailors onboard ship for designated functions in the future.

The CDES facility is located on the Point Loma peninsula, which formed a barrier for the San Diego Bay, facing the Pacific Ocean. The Cabrillo National Monument is located at the Southern tip of the peninsula. If you stand on the end of the peninsula you can get a full view of the Pacific Ocean on the West side and of San Diego Harbor all the way to Mexico on the East side. Juan Rodriguez Cabrillo was the first European to set foot in what is now the West Coast of the United States as he came onto shore in 1542. Juan was a Conquistador and enslaved the Mixtec people in Oaxaca, Mexico and in the Americas. He was born in Spain and was a mariner from Portugal and with Hernan Cortes caused the fall of the Aztec Empire and brought most of Mexico under the rule of the King of Castille and began the Spanish colonization of the Americas. Because I now worked in Point Loma I would often visit his statue over-looking the beautiful San Diego Bay and imagine his 3 ships sailing into the harbor.

Working in San Diego in Point Loma at the CDES facility I was astounded as it was a very guarded facility and I remember the first day I drove up the roads leading to the gate next to road and I looked down toward the ocean where I could see the facility. The guards searched my car with their dogs circling my vehicle as it was the first time I was visiting the facility and issued me a temporary pass to go down to where I would work for the next 5 years I thought. As I tried to enter the building I entered a secured vestibule and I was asked to show my ID which was scanned remotely. They asked my business and who my sponsor was and finally they buzzed me in. I proceeded down the first-floor hallway and I climbed up the stairs to the second floor as I was directed by the guards. At the end of the second floor were another set of guards and they asked me to sign in and they also asked for my ID and called someone, then finally they pushed another button and a huge orange steel door with a width of maybe 3 feet, which was built to not allow microwaves or signals to pass through, started to open to let me into the adjoining hallway. I was told to go to the 3rd floor and to a specific room. Down the hallway I went and up the next set of stairs in front of the what I thought was my new workplace. The door was locked, and I had to hit a buzzer and I was told to step up into this 7 foot entrance which had a camera and I had to show my picture ID and my face and indicated who I was visiting and after they snapped my picture the coordinator inside the laboratory opened the electronic door. Once inside I immediately had an escort who watched me sign in and I looked around at all the Computers and People working in the CDES laboratory. I finally was allowed to go to the room where my supervisor was waiting for me. I followed this procedure every day for 5 years.

I lived in the Point Loma peninsula in a tennis club condominium and I began to enjoy the diversity of San Diego. I connected with old friends, met new friends and I would go to the Old Town Mission of San Diego to enjoy music and the authentic Mexican food. For rich music I would go to Humphreys to listen to concerts on the Yacht Harbor. I drove my car south to Chicano Park located beneath the San Diego-Coronado Bridge in Barrio Logan. I would get out of my car and talk to the predominately Chicano and Mexican American and immigrants of Barrio Logan at the Park. Chicano Park is home to fabulous collections of outdoor murals as is part of the rich history of the surrounding neighborhoods. The Latinos in the neighborhoods had to fight to keep the park from being taken away from them and being developed. While working at CDES on the Point I would venture outside with my co-workers and check out the fast sailboats racing as part of Americas Cup looking out next to the Pacific Ocean. The San Diego Chargers NFL team and the San Diego Padres were the teams that everyone cheered for while in season. I went to the games as often as I could. Ocean Beach, Pacific Beach, Coronado Beach and riding the Red Trolley to the Mexican Border were all part of the things I enjoyed.

I made new friends in San Diego and one of them was Cadillac Greg. Greg lived in a rundown house in the neighborhood of Old Town with his 6-year-old son. His wife had died of a drug overdose, but he was determined to raise his son as best as he could. He used to drive a pink convertible Cadillac through the town of Mission Beach and would park and go surfing with his friend Marco. During the Chargers football games on Sunday he would cruise the streets by Jack Murphy stadium and when he was sure he would find a house and begin parking cars before the game to make enough to buy scalper tickets. He would leave a note with the extra money and plead that they did not turn him in. Sometimes he'd leave them as much as $500 if it was the right property. I asked him once why he never took any of his many girlfriends to the game. He told me; "Dude I'd rather be with my friends who really like football and we can talk about it for years. The girls just want to be seen and besides sooner or later they will break up with me anyway."

Returning back to California and working in San Diego allowed me to take a short plane flight from San Diego to San Francisco and visit my Mother and family in Pittsburg as often as I liked. I would always pick up the San Francisco newspapers and catch up with my favorite columnist Herb Caen who had a unique way describing the everyday life in the City. I would see my boyhood friends in the old neighborhoods, with my first stop being the New Mecca Café'. While in San Diego I played tennis weekly and became an owner of an 18-foot Hobie catamaran which I moored at the Mission Bay Harbor. I would pull up the sails and tighten up the lines as I took it out every other day after leaving the beach shores next to the Bahia Resort Hotel. At times I would meet tourists at the bar at the Bahia and take them for rides in the Bay. I would take 3-mile walks from the foot of Ocean Beach district and end up at the Pacific Beach and stop in for a beer at Lahaina where I often met my friends after a long day's work for Mexican food. The days and evenings were always mild in San Diego. I worked and lived in San Diego for 5 years and for a time I was in Nirvana. I met a Peruvian guy named Jorge who was as mysterious as they come, and he would tell me stories about how he used to live in the jungle. He had a thick accent, never had a job, but somehow through other means he had just enough money to keep himself going. It hardly ever rained in San Diego and when it did I had an open invitation to all I knew to come to my place to barbecue on my porch which had an overhang to prevent getting wet by the rain. And came they did with their steaks, chicken, beer, and it seemed everyone was in shorts and my little 2 bedroom condo would be full of people laughing and enjoying the music watch the replays of the last Chargers football game on my TV as I had my recorder on. I was preparing to purchase a condo in La Jolla until somehow, while I was not watching, I got married.

I had met my future wife, Kitty, a blonde blue-eyed half Welsh, half German woman working at the CDES facility where I worked in Point Loma. She worked a different shift than I did, and our paths would cross for about 30 minutes each day as we worked on different shifts. She was from Buffalo and for over 4 years we would smile at each other and she would listen to my stories of my short romances that would not last. She was in the Navy Reserve and after returning from Hawaii after her reserve duty one weekend for some unknown reason I became smitten by her. The next thing I knew I asked her out to dinner and instead of going to San Diego, I asked her to give me all her money as I changed it to Pesos as we drove across the border to Mexico. I took her to dinner at a restaurant on the Pacific Ocean, about 45 minutes from San Diego, where no-one spoke English, except for her and I. We took a walk on the beach with the waves washing onshore and over the big boulders where we sat. She told me; "Fernando, you seem pretty sure of yourself. I replied, well I am out on a date with you after 4 years, you have no money, you don't speak the language, it's the middle of the night and nobody knows where you are at, so yeah, I'm sure I'm good." Well she told me; "Hey, I'm not so sure about this." And we both laughed.

So then, after 6 months of courtship I was married at the age of 33. And before I knew it after 4 months of marriage, I was headed back to the East Coast to Virginia after arranging a transfer with my company. My new wife Kitty said she missed the seasons and as a young impulsive new husband, I granted her request to leave. This time I had my condo packed by the movers and they loaded my car onto the vehicle transport, and I flew on the airlines to Virginia Beach. Goodbye Pacific Ocean, goodbye Catamaran, goodbye

Old Town, the beach on Coronado Island, and goodbye Mission Beach. I would miss the salsa music in the bars on Cinco De Mayo and my many Latino friends I had made friendships with while living in San Diego. I would lose more than I bargained for as where I was going the faces would stare just a bit longer as they gazed upon my brown skin and wonder who I was.

So, I packed my bags and walked around my Condo on Point Loma I took a final ride to Sunset Cliffs, Old Town, and Pacific Beach. I said goodbye to my friends; Cadillac Greg, Crazy Jorge from Peru, Joe my Sicilian homie, Marco who always lived life fully and went around the World. Living those 5 years in San Diego seemed like a whisper of time, and that's how life is sometimes. My mother loved visiting me in San Diego and I would fly her in to see me and we would walk on the beaches of Pacific Beach on Shelter Island. Later when she became ill and required some heart procedures she stayed with me until I nursed her to health. When I told her that I was moving to the East Coast she gave me a stern look but said no more. I wish she would have.

SUBMARINES AND AIRCRAFT CARRIERS

My new wife who was from Buffalo and missed the seasons and after being married 6 months in San Diego I worked to move to Virginia Beach. I was able to get a transfer to Virginia Beach, in 1989, and initially was assigned to do training for defense contractors and the military. Virginia Beach was a beautiful place next to the Atlantic Ocean and it had many hotels among its waterfront as it was a tourist town. Down the road was Hampton Roads where many of the military services were located. I bought a beautiful home in an older neighborhood with tall trees and was surprised when I used to see the squirrels laying upon the branches due to the heat. However, after 3 months my job changed, and I was asked to assist IBM, General Electric and other companies to remediate failed electronic systems and make a move to Connecticut. While in Connecticut I attended the University of Connecticut's extension classes at Avery Point and made the dean's list. So, as part of my new work assignment I traveled and worked on Naval Ships at the Bath Maine Ironworks Shipyard located on the Kennebec River. When I walked thru the facility I would walk thru and underneath a sign that read "Through These Gates Pass the Best Shipbuilders in the World."

The shipyard was a part of General Dynamics and had been building ships since 1890 and over the years after World War I constructed over 250 Naval combat ships. I was assigned to work on the DDG-51 class ships and repair the sonar interfaces and help with certification of the sonar systems used to track submarines. Many of these sonar systems were also on submarines and depicted in the movie; THE HUNT FOR RED OCTOBER. The first time I went to Bath Maine it was in the heart of the winter month of December. I can remember walking out on the deck with my hot coffee in a styrofoam cup and as I held it in my hand it instantly froze as I watched clumps of ice in the channel. When I informed my engineering leader about it he said it must be warming up otherwise we would not see floating ice. After 6 months I was asked to return to Virginia Beach where I was also to travel to validate the new systems on the ships that were located at the Pascagoula Shipyards in Mississippi including the newest Aircraft Carriers that were being built. If I thought Virginia Beach was hot and humid, Mississippi changed my mind entirely. At the shipyard I had to walk about 1 mile every morning from the parking lot to the pier where I would arrive with my equipment. I had my equipment in a toolbox and it seemed it got heavier and heavier as it would already be 89 degrees in the morning with 100% humidity. They would not let us keep it onboard so back and forth I carried it. I worked about 3 weeks at a time and for sure I lost about 10 pounds every-time I went. I was glad to get back to Virginia Beach as quickly as I could.

Our first home in Virginia. I found out what heat was really about.

Virginia Beach was located in the Tidewater region of Virginia on the Coast. It was home to the Naval Air Station at Oceana, Norfolk Naval Base, Langley Airforce Base, Little Creek Expeditionary Base among others. Saddam Hussein of Iraq invaded the independent country of Kuwait August 2 of 1990 and began occupying that country as part of his plan of greater Iraq. While the country watched President George Bush state in a speech on August 5; "This will not stand, this aggression against Kuwait" I could already feel the tension beginning on the military bases in Tidewater. In the coming weeks I could see supplies being offloaded from the railroad yards, I could see the sea of fatigues worn by servicemen as they arrived, and I would see the contractors working 24x7 on the ships at the shipyards. Already I could see the planes coming in day after day at the Air Bases. I was quietly asked to prepare to take an overseas flight with a military group as they were going to deploy as part of Desert Shield. However, that assignment did not happen, and I never shared it with anyone. The US prepared for war and with the allies of the United Nations Operation Desert Shield begin at the end of August 1990 thru February of 1991 with air bombings. Norfolk and Virginia had strategic Naval and Marine bases and as security increased around the bases and ships in the harbor, I could see the military gearing up to go across the Atlantic Ocean to prepare to stage their forces in Saudi Arabia. I saw closeup the wives scared that their husbands would not return and the child not wanting to let go of their fathers as they boarded the planes and ships.

There were women who were also part of the military and I could see the faces of their husbands and children as they prepared to deploy as well. The liberation of Kuwait and the invasion of Iraq begin on 17 January 1991 and lasted 5 weeks. When the flags of the Iraq regime were brought down and Saddam Hussein was captured, I stood on the grinder on a hill overlooking the air base as I watched the planes returning back to Virginia Beach. My only child, Melissa, was born in April of 1991 and my wife and I decided to move to Buffalo to be next to my wife's parents, as my child was now their only grandchild. In Buffalo I would learn how to layer on my clothes as the cold air could quickly create frostbite with an average snowfall of 100 inches. In Diego it was all shorts and sandals with the average rainfall of 12 inches. In Virginia I was where the humidity was stifling and was so hot and I would feel the temperature wear me out as it would reach 116 degrees with the heat index. But the future is not for the meek and the Chicano from Pittsburg was on his way to the home of blizzards and whiteouts and of course the Buffalo Bills.

BUFFALO, NEW YORK

I prepared for my move to Buffalo in 1990 and to make Western New York my new home. I stayed until 2014. A Latino from Pittsburg living in the snow capital of our country, yeah lets see how this turns out. It was the longest time I had lived anywhere in my life. I had sent my wife and my child to live with my in-laws before I joined them. I was faced with selling my home in Virginia Beach as well as finding employment in a city where I knew absolutely no one. Making a move over 600 miles to uncertainty was risky but I did make it happen and started my own computer consulting practice for 6 months in Buffalo to make myself and my skills known. My friends told me that there was no way I was going to get meaningful computer work in Buffalo, but I had traveled there on vacation visiting my wife's family numerous times and I was confident I could make it on my own. I sent my wife and daughter ahead to live with my in-laws and searched for an apartment. On January 3rd, 1991 we finally found the right place and I moved to the town of Hamburg which was located 2 miles from the Buffalo Bills NFL football stadium. On that day I started to help unpack as I moved into my new apartment and I decided to do that instead of going to the football game nearby. I have regretted that decision ever since.

The Buffalo Bills number 1 QB, Jim Kelly was injured and would not play, their number 1 linebacker Cornelius Bennett was hurt and would not play and their number 1 running back, Thurman Thomas, got hurt early in the game and did not play again. All 3 are enshrined in the NFL Hall of Fame. The Bills did not have a chance, or so everyone said. That football playoff game Is now known as the greatest comeback game ever as the Buffalo Bills overcame a 32-point deficit to the Houston Oilers and won the game in overtime. Many of the fans began leaving the game before halftime but by the end of the 3rd quarter the fans were climbing the fences to get back into the stadium. My beloved Oakland Raiders had moved to Los Angeles in 1982 and I was a Raiders fan until that moment. I would later go the small college in Fredonia 30 miles away to watch the team practice in a small college atmosphere and would share wings with some of the players as they hung out at the Big Tree Inn bar in the town of Orchard Park. In the years that I was in New York I became a Buffalo Sports fan and the Buffalo Bills were my number 1 team.

I worked for 3 companies in New York. The first was Delaware North a $1.5Billion dollar financial holding company, as their lead Computer administrator for their high-tech financial systems and applications. They were known in the Sports world as managing concessions at most of the Baseball Major League Ballparks. I thought I would work at Delaware North until I retired but sometimes lightning can strike and change the way you had envision yourself and what you are doing. In 1996 I had a meeting with John Vitale the director of a smaller manufacturing company named Niagara Envelope located in Buffalo. After a couple of meetings with him he asked for my resume and after reviewing it he asked me this question; "Fernando, can you explain to me which of these projects you managed, and which one did you actually do the work?" After finding out that I was the project lead responsible for defining the projects, scheduling, budgeting, managing resources, reporting and also doing the majority of the transformational changes he took me over to his company and introduced me to his business and technology teams for discussions. He made me an offer I could not refuse and after being under John's leadership and mentoring he helped me to understand that I had another skill; Understanding Business and Future Transformational ideas. John always kept your bar raised on what you could achieve, and he poured his business background and experiences to me as we prepared to take Niagara to the next level. Niagara Envelope was considered to be the country's 2nd largest Envelope manufacturer. However, it was a 3rd generational private company with record profits and huge competition and it was sold within 3 months of my joining the company. I continue to build my relationship with John after leaving Niagara Envelope and seek his mentorship when I need it and we continue to be friends.

I was prepared and was offered a position at Rich Products a $3Billion dollar multi-national company in Buffalo whose founder was Robert Rich the inventor of the first non-dairy whipped topping in 1945. Later he invented the non-dairy coffee creamer and over 80 different food products manufactured and sold all over the world. Some of these products included; Better Creme, used in cakes, deserts, donuts, muffins, shrimp from St. Simons Island in Georgia, French Baguettes, Ciabatta bread, Donuts, Italian Meat balls among others. He along with Clarence Birdseye who invented flash freezing changed the food industry. Rich's also owned PGA National Golf course in Florida and the Triple A team of the New York Mets and I was able to work and provide support for their other entertainment ventures. As part of my role I was part of a team with transforming the company from a mainframe-based environment to newer technologies. One of the most challenging aspects of the position was being successful in executing our Disaster Recovery strategy as we duplicated our business processes and technologies in Philadelphia multiple times to support the business in case our headquarters in Buffalo was hit with a disaster. I was also part of a startup ticketing company as part of a partnership with Rich Products, called Fantastix, with customers like the National Hockey League Buffalo Sabres and the Triple A team of the New York Mets. The ticketing company was sold and eventually become Tickets.com the ticketing company owned by Major League Baseball.

Living in Buffalo was like living in a large town with generations of diverse families with about 30% Polish, 32% German, and 30% Irish as the majority. Everyone seemed to know everybody with the police force comprised of old Irish families, the firefighters comprised of long time Polish families. At one time Buffalo was the 8th largest city in the United States with Bethlehem Steel the predominant employer. The Erie Canal went thru the middle of city with transportation of goods from the East Coast arriving Daily and then put on trans to go the West Coast. Niagara Falls was approximately 20 miles away and Indian Reservations surrounded the towns in and around Buffalo. For a time, there was an NBA Basketball team called the Buffalo Braves which eventually folded and moved to Los Angeles and was renamed the Clippers. There are multiple Colleges with names like St Bonaventure, Niagara, University of Buffalo and produced NBA Stars like Bob McAdoo and Ernie DiGregorio, the French Connection on the NHL Buffalo Sabres and NFL legends Jim Kelly, Thurman Thomas and the infamous OJ Simpson. The Buffalo Bills lost 4 straight Superbowl's in the 90s with the first loss always resonating with "Wide Right" as they missed a field goal at the end of their first Superbowl.

The Buffalo Sabres had the infamous "No-Goal" as they lost the Stanley Cup in the finals to the Dallas team and the city lost their NBA team. But no matter because Sports rules the city and always gives it hope before each season and when their teams fail, there's always next year. The city of Buffalo lies next to the Niagara River and Lake Erie with Canada a 2-minute drive over the Peace Bridge. Niagara Falls lies a 20-minute drive to the North and Toronto 2 hours away by car. The winters are harsh with snowbanks that can reach 7 feet and whiteouts that would leave you dizzy with fear and winters with blizzard winds shutting down all the towns around Buffalo. The infamous Blizzard of 1977 brought the region to a standstill as it hit western New York as well as southern Ontario from Jan 28 to Feb 1. Daily peak wind gusts ranged from 46 to 69 mph and as high as 100 mph in some areas. The high winds blew this into drifts of 30 to 40 ft. Snow began to fall at 5 am and observers on the 16th floor of some buildings began to see a gray sky approaching the city from Lake Erie and turning white from the reflection of the sun. By 11 am the city of Buffalo was beginning to be hit with the high winds and the white walls of snow began tumbling down. The city and surrounding areas with the help of the National Guard survived the event with stories still being told of how the communities helped each other survive the national disaster.

It seemed that everyone had 2 snow-shovels in their trunk of their car and maybe 30% of the trucks on the road had snow blades when they did not take off until June. Once it kept snowing and we accumulated over 7 feet of snow. Took me 7 hours to drive 20 miles from work to home. The mayor of Buffalo was Jimmy Griffin a gruff Irishman who was elected in 1977 and continued to get re-elected until 1993. An Army veteran of the Korean war he was known for his candor. When they asked him what his snow plan was he said "Go home, buy a 6 pack of beer and watch the football games. "This earned him the name of "Jimmy Six Pack." But the City of Buffalo was really a community of different ethnicities living in different wards in the city and to the south-towns and New York western style pizza and wings were everywhere. On Friday's almost in every corner of the surrounding towns people would go to the restaurants and VFW halls and enjoy their Fish Fry dinners and just visit with each other as they talked about the snow, the Bills or Sabres, and their families, in that order.

The City of Buffalo has some of the oldest buildings in the United States with historical Architecture almost on every corner of downtown. As cold as the winters get, and winter can come as early as August and leave by late spring, the people of Buffalo and the hamlets surrounding it exhibit a community of caring like no other city in the World and its population in 2018 was 256,000. It is really a little city or a big town, anyway you want to shake it. Buffalo always seems to have as many festivals in the summer as the ethnicities that populate its wards including the Buffalo Chicken Wing Festival, the German Fest, Hop Harvest Fest, Buffalo Irish Festival, Music Art Festival, Allentown Art Festival, the Clam Fest and many others. The Erie County Fair located in the town of Hamburg has been running since 1820 and when it opens it hosts over 1 million people over a 10 day in August. Driving alongside the Niagara River from Buffalo there are some of the most scenic views of the Niagara Gorge ending up at Niagara Falls. The Ford Automobile Manufacturing Stamping plan in Cheektowaga has often been called "The Mistake on the Lake" as the plan it strongly Unionized and frequently does not approve the changes that Detroit would like them to do. However, it is one of the most efficient plants in operation turning out high quality work.

I purchased a home in Hamburg, 20 miles from the City and two miles from the Buffalo Bills stadium. I would frequently go the football games and tailgate with my friends during the games and at times I would go into the Big Tree Inn during the week and a lot of times the Buffalo Bills players would be there playing darts, eating pizza and chicken wings and telling stories with the people in the bar. I will always treasure my time in Buffalo as I made many friends and of course had some people who just couldn't get over who I was. I purchased a home 20 miles from Buffalo in the town of Hamburg, which was located about 3 miles from the Buffalo Bills stadium and it was there in Hamburg where my daughter Melissa started her young life with her many good friends.

When my daughter was about 6 years old she started to enjoy the sport of Volleyball. She was a Libero and would set up the front line, medium line girls for their spikes to gain points. But she was also a very strong server. Maybe because she was a bowler, but she could toss the ball over her head and pop it hard right over the net. Sometimes she would be afraid that she would hurt someone if it hit them. She was a competitor but also was compassionate to others. I was working with a team of about 25 people for our first disaster recovery exercise in the City of Philadelphia. It was winter and we sent our data tapes to the facility, which was located in a bad section of town and we created an enormous amount of documentation and did many sub-tests to prepare under the leadership of my friend Joe Ventura, an old school IT mainframe veteran from the city of Buffalo. To get our people to be ready as a team Joe took us to Maggiano's a famous Italian Restaurant where we ate all we could and enjoyed the best wines that Joe could identify. The next we begin our setup and data recovery and communicated with the 3 floors of computers using a radio and based on a schedule. I took the lead on the Unix Systems and was asked to work with the Mainframe and other teams a key facilitator. In most companies' disaster recovery testing in a remote city normally ends in failure, but we were focused and ready to succeed. On the 2nd night I was in the Computer Control room when someone said; "Fernando you got an urgent phone call from home. "I thought the worse. They patched it to me at the Center and sure enough it was my young daughter Melissa who was at a Volleyball Tournament. "Dad, we did it, we did it, we won. We were behind by 8 points and I served and got 10 points in a row. "I said to her; "Mija thanks for calling me and don't ever forget this feeling, you made my day. OK Mija I have to go, take care of your Mom and celebrate with your friends." My friends laughed and said; "Can we go now?". And we did and we were successful. Our teams in Buffalo would remote login to the system and run a series of reports to ensure the data was accurate. Of course, we recovered the systems with an older date but never-the-less we did it. I had great friends and colleagues that made it successful, but I also knew that I was the only Latino that was part of this team.

It Was All About the Data. The one thing I learned early about technology and systems was that no matter how fast your system was, or how reliable it was, the most critical part of the system was its data. Sooner or later you would need to be able to restore and recover that data to within a minute of its change.

After just getting home late on Friday the head of Operations asked me to check the systems as our company was at a standstill as our newly transformed major application, called SAP, was not working right. We had transitioned from the Mainframe systems used for over 20 years to this new SAP environment, also used by Volkswagen and Boeing, in 9 months. A minor miracle. After I assured them that the systems were validated I looked through the logs and advised them that the issue was related to the application. They then began calling all the applications teams together and said goodbye to me. The time was 5:30 PM. I received a call at 4:30 AM and was asked to come in. I asked them to turn off a specific scheduled job before I left. When I arrived, I saw the haggard and tired looks of most of my department, my Director, my CIO and the owner of the company pacing next to our consulting experts from IBM. They asked if there was anything I could do. I asked my recovery expert how many windows he had open while trying to recover the data and he told me, about 25. That shook me. I took over the lead to resolve the issue, called one of our consulting partners and a friend I had faith in. The key here is that it was all about the data. Our data was part of a massive Oracle relational database. If I could not solve the problem and identify how to recover the data then our 3 Billion company would be at risk. I was prepared as I designed the system to automatically mirror our data daily in case our systems went down and our recovery tapes were not available. I also took the time to document what I considered a disaster scenario and documented the data recovery procedures for myself. I was able to be successful with the help of my key friend and my recovery manager, Paul Thurston, and we made some critical decisions along the way, which we shared to the astonishment to our teams later. We recovered the data to within 5 minutes of when the problem first showed itself caused by a consultant from IBM who made a bad decision and kicked off a feature to have the system continually import all the changes we had implemented for configurations, over 2,500, and that's why the symptoms continually were changing. I definitely earned my keep that day and my knowledge of technology, database recovery and our business processes helped me recover our business data.

I later asked one of our senior managers how it was that I was called in and he said to me "I asked Sellito to call you and he said Sandoval, he is Infrastructure what can he do. Then he answered him, he's never let me down and he always seems to have a horseshow up his a…." In any case no one ever thanked me or gave me special recognition. After a post discussion with IBM, our team, and a few others I remember going down an escalator and a senior staff colleague yells from above the escalator yells down to me, as I was at the bottom; "Fernando, by the way, could you tell me what your Nationality Is?" I looked back up the escalators and saw the quizzical looks on the people coming down awaiting my reply and I coolly answered back; "I'm American, How about you". Then he followed up with "That's not what I meant", and I responded before walking out the door; "Really, well what did you mean". I had a conversation with this individual after lunch. I was 45 years old and the lesson was not lost on me, there will be some people that will think you are not American enough or good enough. "No matter where you go, there you are, and there they are. "

I received a call one day and it was my father who had been living in Mexico in the state of Nayarit. He had been searching for me for over 40 years. I had never met him and with the help of his sister and nephew he was finally able to locate where I was and made the connection. So I went to the mountains of Nayarit in Mexico for 2 weeks and within a few days I started to slowly see my father's zest for life and he took me to the small town that he grew up in and the original small casa that he lived in, which to this day still had no electricity. He spoke multiple languages and was involved politically in his small town and I watched him capture the attention of the other men as he spoke. He had a quick wit and a hearty laugh and enjoyed a full meal. I started to understand where my personality came from as he continued to show me his world and introduced me to his family.

Nayarit, by my Father's house. Waiting on the milk to be delivered.

Sadly, he would soon start feeling the onset of Alzheimer's after his heart became weak and a pacemaker was installed in his chest. I could see his quick walk slow down to a small gait. Before the Alzheimer's set in he was a fearless driver on the narrow mountain roads to his house on Piedras Negras in Nayarit. As we traveled on the road we would see the small memorials of those who had died trying to navigate and perish to their death. I saw my father multiple times in the nursery homes as he got worse and my sister Gracie brought her guitar and sang to him and he responded to the music and the words. Even though I did not know him long I am my father's son.

A TUESDAY I WILL NEVER FORGET- 9/11

My work normally started at 8 AM but one morning, as I was working for Rich Products, I came into Buffalo at about 8:45 as I and a few others were to meet at a historical building across the street, called the Green House, for Human Resources training. It was September 11, 2001. The Green House was used as part of the Pony Express, the overland company that used teenagers to go across the company on special Pony's to deliver the mail and money. It was a sunny morning and as I pulled into the parking lot I was about to turn off my car radio when I heard the following; "It has been reported a small plane has hit the World Trade Center." I was stunned somewhat but I did not understand the magnitude at that moment. As soon as walked into the room in the Green House with my colleagues seated we were asked to turn off all cell phones, all beepers and put our computers away. We were to be isolated for the next 2 hours with no interruptions as HR conducted their training. When the training was over we were in a festive mood and we all start walking across the street to 1150 Niagara Street, the HQ of Rich Products to enter the main building. As I entered the building I saw additional security at the front door and maybe 25 people transfixed on the main television in the center of the room.

Before I could fathom what was happening I was witnessing the first tower of the World Trade Center disintegrating and falling into the Street of New York City. Everyone was quiet and then I heard one of the senior lawyers say; "All We Need is a Target, Get us a Target". I walked up the stairs to gather with all the rest of my team and rumors were flying everywhere. They let me know what had been happening over the last 2 hours and I knew immediately that everything had changed. I called my friend who had just been to the Towers recently working with the Computer Systems guys for the companies in the Tower. I remember him speaking to me on the phone and saying. "There could have been 50,000 people in the Towers and now they're Gone, Gone Gone." No one knew exactly how many people were in the Towers and that many had evacuated at that moment. There were 412 Fireman and Police killed trying to help those who were killed in the Towers and they were part of the 2,977 victims on that fateful day. I was in shock and our directors asked us to stay because they were not sure what other cities were going to be attacked. I stayed until 7 in the evening, along with about 75 of my colleagues, transfixed on the televisions that were brought out. When I got home I just could not stop watching my television and did not fall asleep until 3 in the morning. I had friends who worked in the Towers and had met them over the years and on that day I knew they were gone.

Many of the companies in the Towers had their backup computer systems and their data in the other Tower. Some of them did not recover. A friend of mine was asked to recreate the computer systems to allow for electronic trading as part of the Instinet system. The existing computers were now all gone. He had to go through the new security with daily searches, questions as he entered ground zero. The computers he needed were no longer made and he made a request all over the country for the parts he needed. Old monitors began flooding in with post-it notes still on them, pictures of their kids and computer boards. Trading was able to be resumed one week later and he was put on the medical watch list for future issues. Another friend of mine from EMC Corporation, the World's largest Data company, was giving a seminar at the Marriott. Just as he began the beepers started going off in the audience. He said half the audience quickly and quietly exited. He then heard a boom about 15 minutes later and then the beepers started going off again in the audience and the other half of the audience started noisily to leave. The security guards came in and frantically told everyone that they had to leave. As my friend walked out the door of the Marriott Hotel he saw some of the bodies falling as he looked up toward the Towers. He ran and could not find a cab then he went to the Subways and the metro had stopped them all. He then ran to the Ferry on Battery Street and cowered in a seat as it took in so many people and it went over the harbor to New Jersey. I remember reading about World War I/II and Korea and those events did not belong to me, they belonged to my parents.

On that day on 9/11 the FAA stopped all air traffic in the United States. Two weeks later I flew from Buffalo to Manhattan once air travel was allowed and I waited in the security line for approximately 1 hour before I arrived at my gate. When I arrived at my gate I noticed that no one was there, and I went the adjoining gate to ask where the attendants and people where. When they found out my name they alerted security and took me to a room to be frisked. They were not sure who I was and only knew that I my luggage needed to be taken off the plane and also the passengers because I was not on the plane. Once all the security people researched who I was an got clearance they put me on another plane to New York City. As I took my seat on the plane I noticed that I was 1 of only 5 passengers onboard and surmised that at least one of the others worked as part of the new Transportation Security Authority.

On Oct 30, 2001 I went to New York and to Yankee Stadium for game 3 of the World Series. It was only 49 days after the attacks. The country was still recovering from 9/11 but I was invited by a colleague who had friends who had perished in the Towers. I remember being downtown, walking outside my Hotel, and standing outside a bar across the street which was surrounded by approximately 15 police officers. As I peered in I could see a family all alone quietly eating dinner. As I looked closer I could see that it was Tino Martinez the star first baseman of the New York Yankees. I took the train to Yankee Stadium located in the Bronx and I could hear the chatter, the profanity, and the hopes from the fans from Brooklyn as we felt the wobble of the train on the trestle. Yankee Stadium was located only a few miles from Ground Zero. Once the train stopped we walked down the stairs and were scanned, went through 2 metal detectors and was frisked again as we went through security. President Bush was going to throw the first pitch and tension was in the air. As he came out from the dugout onto the field and to the pitcher's mound you could clearly see he was wearing a bullet proof vest. Everyone in the stadium stood up and gave the loudest cheers for the President and for our country. The secret service was at every entrance and corner of the ballpark. The game in a nail-biter with Roger Clemens of the Yankees having one of his better games giving up only 3 hits and striking out 9. The Yankees had lost the first 2 games but won the game that night and the sellout crowd in Yankee Stadium roared as the Yankees started their comeback and eventually took the World Series Championship from the Arizona Diamondbacks. Vietnam in 1975, the Gulf War in 1990/1991 and September 11 in 2001 were all part of my history. That day in 2001 and those memories will last a lifetime.

FROM BUFFFALO TO SWITZERLAND

Someone I was becoming the expert on the systems that I maintained, and my companies continued to send me to advanced training for emerging technologies. I learned how to manage projects from $10,000 to 250,000. Not many get the chance to lead organizations for change. I heard about Hersey doing a project for over a year and spending millions and even then it failed. The project manager was blamed and fired. The last job in Buffalo which I held from 2007 to 2014 was with the HSBC Bank, which was headquartered in Buffalo and had assets and liabilities in the U.S. of over $200Billion Dollars. It is part of an International bank with its headquarters based on Canary Wharf in London, England. I had originally been assigned with work with Engineering and was assigned to oversee the computing systems to support the Finance Function of the Bank. I was asked to shadow a difficult project that had been going on for 18 months in which 3 project managers were fired and 2 quit. I was asked what recommendations I could provide to turn the project around. The next thing I knew I was being introduced to the teams in Buffalo, Chicago and support personnel in India as the new project manager. I submitted my revisions to the plan, on this project that was already 1 year behind schedule and had exhausted its budget. My boss was fearful that it could not be saved, but I made it happen with the great team of people once I gained their trust. I was then reclassified as the relationship manager for Finance and oversaw all the projects in their portfolio. It was an important position the functions of Finance were at the heart of Banking as they managed all the data for all the customers that had deposits and did business with the bank. I was fortunate to complete successfully all the projects I was given for the US Bank and because I had a deep technology background they ensured I was asked to take over assignments that were considered the most complex and I directed the consulting firms of Deloitte, Anderson Consulting and others help complete them..

I was then assigned as a Global Relationship Manager with work with Wholesale Credit, Risk, Compliance, Consumer Mortgage Lending, Global Banking and Markets, and the Private Bank as I worked with HSBC Banking subsidiaries around the World as part of my leadership on the Asset Liability Function. Leading this function was almost overwhelming and required an enormous amount of travel and training to keep up with regulations that were part of the Bank Secrecy Act, Anti-Money Laundering, Financial Crimes Compliance, Mortgage Processes, and Reporting, among others. I had to become an expert on designs, process and systems that were created over a period of 30 years. As HSBC Bank had affiliate Banks in over 80 distinct locations and internationally in the Middle East, Asia, Europe, North and South America I had to understand the Regulatory rules for each region and work with Information Technology teams around the world. I would frequently travel to Toronto Canada and meet with our business and technology teams as we prepared to update our systems and move their data into our cloud. It would take 2 hours to drive from Buffalo to Toronto and if you did not know the way you would quickly get lost as the signage on the roads were poor. And everyone drove fast, faster than you could imagine as the signs for speed was in kilometers and for the life of me I could not feel comfortable on those roads. Toronto was beautiful as it was the capital of the province of Ontario and I enjoyed the English Architecture and enjoyed dinner at the CN Tower where you could see the city from above and enjoyed the NHL Hockey Hall of Fame.

One day my business partner, Chuck Bellavia called me from London, and asked me if I could join him in England to help in supporting the transformation we were planning for Banks in London, Paris, the Middle East, and Switzerland. This assignment would last 4 months and right before I left I got a call that a Volcano erupted in Iceland. Air travel was started to be restricted so I had to hurry to travel from New York to London. On the way I could see the massive effects of the Volcano in the skies and the pilot diverted us over Greenland to ensure we were not captured in the storm. Once I arrived I could already see the chaos in the streets as business was heading to a standstill because no one was coming into London and there was beginning to be food shortages and materials and workers. I met with the heads of the ALM functions and technical leaders of the countries we were working with. It was a strict environment with only the brightest at the bank invited to work there. Suit and Tie all the way. There were over 300,000 employees in HSBC around the world in 2010 with approximately 40,000 located in the United Kingdom. I remember the first time I was walking on Canary Wharf in the heart of the Finance Center among the many people in London and looked up at the 45 story HSBC Tower and pinched myself because I never thought I would be in a place like this.

My expertise had evolved from being a senior project manager in engineering to working with business as an internal consultant and being assigned to large critical business projects. I became a project management professional with training on resource management scheduling, reporting, risk, and budgeting. The had to provide constant reports to our business teams, our Chief Information Officer, and our technology partners. Working at HSBC I became immersed in the regulations of the Bank Secrecy Act, Anti-Money Laundering, Regulatory Reporting, Compliance and how the businesses worked together. I would be part of review teams and discuss how to prevent bad actors (cartels, dictators) from leveraging banks to hide their money. Even banks had bad actors and tried to find a way around the regulations and reporting. If we as citizens had been caught laundering money we would go to jail, surely. However, the big banks with their connections and role in the world were only fined for doing this and for the most part no one went to jail. I will explore this in another book. The story still has not been told. I had been successful in the US and now I was asked to work with the stars at the bank who were working in London. I walked through the iconic large HSBC Lions on each side of the Main Entrance. After going through security my sponsor came down from the 34th floor to greet me and take me the indoctrination office so I could be on-boarded. Even though I had been working for HSBC in New York I was now in another country and I had to fill-out many new forms, have my fingerprints and my picture taken. This took all of the first day and on the 2nd day I began joining in on Conference calls with my colleague Charles as we talked to many heads of departments in reviewing the plans of the week and the day. This happened on a daily basis, and one custom that I was not prepared for was the Noon hour. At Noon EVERYONE in the bank left to go to lunch. No one was left behind. Because HSBC was a world bank there were races from all over the world working in the building. Everyone spoke English; however, the twist was that they spoke it with their native accents. I met colleagues from Hong Kong, Poland, Dubai, Saudi Arabia, the continent of Africa to name a few. The culture in London is to ensure that when you work you take your lunch hour as if it was a requirement that had to be adhered to. Leaving the building I was introduced to the street vendors and had fish and chips in a rolled-up newspaper. When in Rome as they say.

While working in London I lived about 4 blocks away and stayed on the 4th floor of an apartment overlooking the Thames River with my colleague Charles from New York. We were diehard Buffalo Bills and Buffalo Sabre fans and we would stay up late after work having a drink and looking for the London channel for the news updates on both of those teams. While in London I visited Westminster Abbey, an historical gothic abbey church which was designated to be a royal monastery and a place for coronations and burial of monarchs. In the Abbey there a number of effigies of famous royal family members. The funeral of Princess Diana was held at the Abbey and the weddings of both of her sons, Prince William and Prince Harry, were also held there. Sir Isaac Newton and Charles Darwin are royal figures that have buried in the Abbey. I talked to many of the older people in London and they would tell me stories about the siege in London in World War II which was known as the London Blitz with nighttime bombings by the Nazi when the populace would hide out in shelters underground. The Tube or the London Underground is a public rapid transit system in London and its connected to cities with 270 stations served. I would be underground as far as 300 feet and hear the winds of the trains echoing. I traveled to Cambridge and at the University saw closeup the artifacts of Charles Darwin. The city of Cambridge is full of University and colleges and is unique with bicycles

136

everywhere for the populace. The streets are narrow to a fault and you cannot drive cars everywhere so bicycles are the primary form of transportation.

One evening I was invited to a party by one of our colleagues from the Bank. My friend Chuck and I took the elevator down from his flat and walked a few blocks and hailed a black cabbie to take us to our destination. Once we arrived we up the stairs of an old building and as we entered the apartment of the party I quickly noticed that the guests, who must have numbered over 40, just by listening to their accents while they were having conversations were from different countries. My friend Chuck were the only Americans. There were people there from Spain, Poland, Hungary, Africa, New Zealand, Romania, and Czechoslovakia, among the other counties. I was startled as one of the guests handled me a large beer in a frosted mug and said to me; "Hey mate, let's have a piss and down it as fast as we can!" I started laughing and after only downing maybe 1/3 of the glass of beer I asked him; "What's your hurry, we got all night!" He was about 6 foot 2 inches tall and about 220 pounds and he laughed and said in an accent from down under; "I'm in training mate and I need to keep it going." His name was Hylton and he told me that he had skied over the North Pole the last year and he had was back in training for his next venture. I asked him; "So what are you going to do next?" He finished off his beer and got another one and he said; "Well I was on the North last year and this next year I am skiing over the South Pole!". I said come on, there's no way. He said; "Yes not only is there a way but I have no choice as the bet is on!". I got to know him, and he told me he was in the special forces from New Zealand that he was one of the extreme guys who did this kind of stuff and only worked in banking from time to time to fund his ventures. Quite an interesting guy and he said I was the first Latino he had ever met. I met another guy who was a movie producer from Italy, and it seemed like all the people in the party were over-achievers, so I had no idea why I was invited. But regardless, it was a great time.

During my last month I flew from London to Geneva Switzerland join our Private Bank affiliate. The flight from London to Geneva was quick and even before landing in Geneva I was treated like someone special by the flight attendants. As we got our luggage we took a public transportation train into the city right up to our hotel. Paying was on the honor system. Our hosts quickly arrived at our hotel and gave us a tour of the city. Geneva was broken into two parts, Old Geneva and the newer cosmopolitan part. It was full of banks from around the world. We walked into Old Geneva on the cobblestone streets up through the hills of the town. We entered into a small passageway of Saint Peters Cathedral, which was the symbol of Christian Reformation. As we continued our walk there were monuments to old generals and their solders as they walked through the city. Julius Cesar and his legions occupied Switzerland as he tried to take over France. France had brought in their armies annexed Switzerland in the late 1700s. Napoleon tried to rule the people, but the people resisted with many coup d etats. Eventually the Swiss prevailed and became an independent nation. Geneva was extra clean, and it seemed that all the cars were freshly washed. Geneva was known for its chocolates and it did not disappoint. We had a meeting at the Wilson House, named for Woodrow Wilson, and which was used as the first meeting place of the League of Nations.

Geneva, Switzerland, from Old Geneva

The HSBC Private Bank, where I was working, was where the wealthiest people of the world stored their money away from the scrutiny of the countries in which they lived. Herve Falciani in 2008, a former IT employee, saved some archived data files and revealed the abuse of tax evasions being done all over the world and sent it to the press. A French court sentenced him to 5 years in prison for industrial espionage. HSBC had to agree to work with different countries including the United States, Argentina, France, Switzerland to undercover its money laundering and tax evasion schemes in its Private Bank in Switzerland and faced up to 1.5Billion dollars in fines. HSBC Holdings in 2017 agreed to pay over 353 million dollars to settle the investigation of tax evasion by its French citizens. While in Switzerland I worked with a colleague who was from Spain to oversee the changes necessary to keep the Private Bank institution open amidst the investigations and audit by the European Regulatory. I was stunned as I went to the International Red Cross, which was headquartered in Geneva, and saw the thousands and thousands of index cards in containers across the entire basement for the prisoners of war throughout history. All the wars and battles throughout history which were displayed on its 4 walls and surrounded the entire basement. That was sad to see. As I walked across the bridge to old Geneva I was able to walk see the plaques where the generals of the Roman Empire battled to take over the city and where the French ruler Napoleon brought his armies. When I returned to New York I left HSBC and took a position as a consultant for Capital Markets, with headquarters in Belgium, to provide services as required to its banking customers.

During that Christmas I received a call from my sister saying my mother was going to go the hospital for surgery and not to worry as she did not think she would be in there long. But my mother did not rebound as the doctors expected and finally my sister called me and told me to hurry. I got on the first plane from Buffalo and flew to San Francisco. I rushed to the hospital, but she could no longer wait for me and passed, 20 minutes before I arrived. She passed one week before her birthday. I know my Moms last words were "Mijo, ya me voy." We had services for my Mom in the church I had my first communion and we traveled to Mexico to have her ashes buried with my grandmother and grandfather, per her wishes. During her ash internment I had one of the local Mariachi bands play for her as the father said her last rites. I was glad she was back on her tierra and I gathered with our families in Ensenada to celebrate her life and what she had meant to all of us. I stayed for a few days and walked the sandy beach where my grandfather used to take us when we were so young. But I had to return to Florida and I made my way back to Pittsburg.

After over 20 years in New York I had moved to the West Palm Beach, Florida due to my wife's failing health condition and worked remotely using the technology of VPN to communicate with my teams in the United States and over the world, and traveled time to time to New York as needed. Upon graduation from College my daughter Melissa joined us in Florida and began her first job. Her life was just beginning, and my life was transforming. With my Mom's passing and also my Father's I felt like an orphan. I really did not know anyone in Florida, and I tried my best to embrace where I was. I had a huge house, lived close to my mother-in law, and the ocean. I looked to find the secret taco trucks in West Palm Beach for my favorite foods and if I was lucky I would be in the warmth of those speaking Spanish. But like someone had told me once, I had less Christmas's in my future than my past.

CORPORATE AMERICA

So, from my beginnings living in the labor cannery camp town of Isleton, teaching myself English and walking through the streets of Pittsburg in my youth surviving the chaos of the 60s and early 70s, mowing lawns, delivering newspapers and digging ditches in the heat of Camp Stoneman I had no idea what lay ahead. But I was confident. My friends went to college, got jobs in the steel mill or went to jail. I fell into the age of technology, went to Vietnam, and saw the world. I read about the Manhattan project and ending up supporting Nuclear testing and top-secret research at Lawrence Livermore National Laboratory. I was setting my path to begin my journey in Corporate America. Late in my career I did attend the University of Connecticut and State University of New York, but that a smaller part of my education.

My career has taken me from Livermore to Los Angeles, Rhode Island, Minneapolis, San Diego, Connecticut, Virginia Beach, New York, Mississippi, and Maine. So many places in so many states. It was actually ironic as growing up we did not have a car to even drive from Pittsburg to Concord. I became an infrastructure system engineer installing and integrating computers, networking, security, performance management, disaster recovery and involved in business resumption and became a Systems Architect helping design high performance models. I became an expert of relationship databases, Unix based systems, distributed systems and worked on Mainframe systems. I was fortunate to work on the emerging technologies of the times with leading companies; Sperry Rand in Minnesota and Rhode Island, Hughes Aircraft in San Diego, as well as Cisco, Oracle, IBM, EMC, SUN, and Digital Equipment Corporation. I was the lead technologist for a $175 million Envelope manufacturing company in New York and Dallas, a $2 Billion Food company in New York and a $3 Trillion company headquartered in London. I managed the computers for a start-up ticketing company named Fantastix, with our first act being Neil Diamond, which was sold to major league baseball and renamed Tickets.com. As the years passed and as some the technologies of the times became older I also was becoming an OG, along with my friends. But those technologies are still the foundation of many companies in Corporate America, but the new technologies of tomorrow will take us on the mission to Mars.

What I learned the most about Corporate America is that the opportunities were there if you took risks. If you took the risks you could be a rising star, but it only took one bad deed to have it all come tumbling down. The higher you went in organizations the more competitive it would become. I was lucky to make many friends, mentors, and sponsors as I was asked to take on more because it was needed. There was no room for second best as they wanted the best and you could be replaced if you went from being called value add to useful. The key was continuous training, connecting with successful people and teams and doing more than they thought you could. I had discovered that due to technology, the need to distribute our likes and dislikes, and the impact of social media that 90 percent of the data that is available has been created in the last year. Moore's Law used to state that the performance of computers would double every 18 months. According to IBM, the doubling of knowledge will happen every 12 months and in the future it will accelerate to every 12 hours. This is due to the buildout of the internet of things.

But the constant to manage this incredible change in the future is people. Over all the years I did feel the implicit discrimination that others grew up with, but for the most part I overcame that by connecting on a personal level with so many. I had my detractors, but I bypassed them by taking higher challenges and producing when they thought I could not. But that's the way of the world. But the most important part of my journey was the people. I learned the customs and worked with colleagues in Mexico, Canada, London, Dubai, Hong Kong, India, and Switzerland. The staff at the Research Lab for the Department of Energy showed the way to greatness and I was fortunate to work with so many inspirational people and I excelled in their shadows. Throughout the years I became one of the best at what I did, because I worked with the best. My success is owed to them. I received so much more than I gave as I joined local organizations such as Rotary and Habitat for Humanity to help others. As part of Rotary I was involved in the student exchange program and hosted young students from the Canary Islands and Denmark. The principles that I used in Rotary I used in business and everyday life. They were called the four-way test: "1. Is it the truth? 2. Is it fair to all concerned? 3. Will it be beneficial to all concerned? 4. Will it build goodwill and friendships?" I would visit my hometown of Pittsburg to see my Mom, family and old friends, but time took some of them away. From tortilla chips to computer chips, I have achieved more than I could have ever imagine.

BACK TO THE BURG

After leaving Pittsburg when I was 17 and having moved over 22 times throughout my lifetime I was preparing to leave West Palm Beach with its heat and palm trees and return home after 40 years of being away. Due to the change in technology I could work from home as I spoke to my managers and teams located throughout the world as part of my project manager role. In 2005 Thomas Friedman wrote the book; "The World is Flat." It meant that the rest of the world was catching up to the United States in so many industries and with the advent of the internet, virtual private networks, and the need for companies to reduce costs that our competition was no longer local, but global. I felt that firsthand as we outsourced many of our technology programming needs to India during the Year 2000 scare. Companies then begin to use those remote resources, at much lower cost, as part of their strategic plans. Technology played a big part in that. The consulting company that I was working with had many of its team working from small offices distant from their customers. Sooner or later even McDonalds would have their order takers located in the Philippines via the Internet. Real Estate agents and lawyers could have their work done overseas at a fraction of the cost. Technology was continually changing and so was my personal life.

I had been married for 26 years and had taken my wife and my only daughter with me on trips to Bath Maine, Connecticut and New York. Our last stop was Florida and after I purchased what I thought was our last home things took a different path. My ex-wife was a great Mom for our daughter, and I will always thank her for that, but she had a different journey she wanted to take, for her own reasons, and she wanted to take it without me. With that, my marriage dissolved and became a part of my past. After speaking with my daughter, who had recently graduated from college, she agreed that I should come back to be with my family, my town, and my people. Vietnam, Buffalo, Chicago, New York City, Geneva were all behind me as part of my past life. When I first came back I had flown to San Diego, visited with friends and enjoyed the calm waters of Mission Bay. I rented a car and began to make the drive by myself from San Diego, past San Clemente enjoying the mountains to the East and the Ocean on the West side of highway 5 and passed through the mission at San Juan Capistrano. It was a late fall day and I broke up my loneliness by listening to oldies music on the Sirius station. I drove through Los Angeles and over the Grapevine mountains through the Tejon Pass and took highway 99, which runs from the Calexico next to the Mexican border north to the state of Washington.

Highway 99 has always been one of my favorites as its next to the towns and cities of the working class stretched with orchards and farmland. As I went North across the central valley I remembered so vividly the days of Cesar Chavez and the farmworkers struggle. Delano, Pixley, Tulare, Visalia, Fresno were etched in my memory. As in the 60s many growers today continue the abuse of the workers.

As I continued my drive to the San Joaquin Valley in the Central Coast of California and passed the farmlands I would stop at times and pull over and walk towards the workers stripping the fields of its crops. Many of these fields are owned by large corporations and they continually to depress wages by hiring undocumented workers to compete with migrant workers who are largely ethnic Mexican Americans. I was one of those workers when I was young helping my family in the summers. As I got close to home I drove on the 4-lane road over the hill on highway 4, which we used to call Blood Alley when it was a dangerous 2-way road when I was growing up, and past the Naval Weapons Station. I would see the twin hills overlooking Mount Diablo and I knew I was home. Port Chicago, next to West Pittsburg, was the home of the infamous weapons explosion in 1944 with over 4,600 tons of munitions detonated in a fire seen for miles. All 320 men on the pier died instantly and 390 others were injured. It was a story that has often been repeated so that we never forget.

I was going back to so many memories and the land of Chicanos I thought. I passed West Pittsburg and now was renamed Bay Point I could see the BART trains on my left as I took the exit heading North on Bailey road. I saw some childhood friends as I went to the New Mecca café and they greeted me; "Fernando, hey are YOU back was their quizzical question?" I smiled and said yes as I found a quiet booth and was served the infamous bean dip that I had always enjoyed as a child. I have been all over the world and worked with so many and as they say here "You can never really leave the Burg, no matter where you go!" But now Pittsburg was different in so many ways and it seemed like I was on a new journey of discovery as I reconnected with the town that took care of me when I was growing up.

Now I understood. No matter where I went or what I achieved, I needed to return.

I drove on the streets where I used to do my paper routes and walked downtown across Cutter Street and toward Montezuma and East to the river as I remembered so many of the friends in the neighborhoods who were now a memory of my past.. At times I did not recognize the neighborhoods because they had torn down the houses where I lived and segregated the streets as part of new developments. With development the community feeling for me on my old streets had disappeared. I walked through the streets of my youth; On 3rd Street across to Cutter Street and to the end on West Santa Fe next to the BSNF railroad tracks. It seems ironic that now there is a 2-level chain link fence over 10 feet tall with barb wire circulating the top of the fences that separate the downtown barrio from the rest of Pittsburg. As I walked upon the broken cement walkways and potholes that lined the street on Black Diamond I thought it was ironic as I also lived and walked among the Palm Trees in West Palm Beach and walked the cobblestone streets in Geneva, Switzerland. No matter what I have achieved there will always be those in poverty and in need, even in the roots of my hometown. Many people ask me why I continue to be active and help and I can only answer that how can I not help.

Coming back home, the bowling alleys had closed, the Green Onion record store looked like it never existed, Rexall, Payless, Sols, Anitas and the Kleins stores were a distant memory. Camp Stoneman was no longer empty as it was filled with housing, apartments and business. The nearby farming towns of Oakley and Brentwood with their orchards and fields I almost did not recognize as now they grew from a population of 2,000 to over 40,000. I met with my good friend Paul Ramirez and I felt like Rip Van Winkle waking up in a new world. I asked him what happened. The Centro on West 8th Street which was used by local Latinos for help with taxes, work, and many other services was gone. The United Council of Spanish Speaking Organizations was now a memory. Al's Hot Dogs at the City Park was gone as was Carlos Pizzeria. The tiendas that were in every neighborhood were a distant past. The city of Pittsburg which used to host parades and fiestas in the park with the smell of grilled corn and the Latino music had changed. The new Latinos were from Guatemala, El Salvador, Nicaragua and other Central American countries had brought their culture and flavorful food to Pittsburg along with their love of soccer. Pittsburg has been re-born but progress has its price and there are still many in poverty in pockets throughout the town.

I was inspired by Paul Ramirez, my old friend, head of the East County United Latino Voices. I became involved with the Martin Luther King March and Cesar Chavez March and tributes with the honorable Gregory Osorio. I became a founding member of Gateway Rotary with my good friend, Danny Lopez, a long-time organizer. I became chairman of the PUSD Bond Oversight Committee to support the modernization and rebuilding of the Schools in Pittsburg. As part of United Latino Voices, I worked with many Latinos in our community for DACA and other issues important to our communities.

Me, Osbaldo Garcia, Oliba Cardona, Danny Lopez, Gregory Osorio

I facilitated a seminar for the Contra Costa Hispanic Chamber of Commerce; "Narrowing the Gap in Education" at Los Medanos College attended by over 350 high schoolers from Antioch, Pittsburg, Oakley, Brentwood, Clayton and Walnut Creek and reconnected with the young. There are so many Latinos that I know that have crossed over the rubicon and have achieved success and are quietly enjoying the fruits of their struggle and education. Many have served in Vietnam, Iraq, and Afghanistan and have earned respect for their contributions. I became renewed as I returned to Pittsburg, really a place I never left. But a new reality was starting to rise as the politics of the day began to stir the racism of the past as part of our new world. "The Future is Now" is a phrase coined by George Allen, head coach of the Washington Redskins. I cannot change the world, but I can advocate for change and help educate the young about the past, the present and to prepare for the future.

THE FUTURE

Working in Corporate America, going to Vietnam, working in Asia, Europe and the Africa I learned firsthand that segregation and discrimination seems to exist everywhere. It is not only endemic to the United States. The Pilgrims fled Europe so that they could have freedom of religion, thought, and life. It has not been perfect, but we are an imperfect nation. I am American by birthright, Latino as part of my Ethnic culture, and Chicano by choice. I acknowledge the repression of the past, the injustice of the present, but I also understand that we can change. There are many who believe the Chicano movement has outlived its radicalism and its usefulness as part of the Latino culture in the United States. Many Latinos have made gains in the economic sector and Hispanics as a whole have registered to vote in many numbers. But overall those are quiet gains and there is a continuing backlash on the gains that were made over the last 50 years as Latinos continue to be a larger portion of the population. There will always exist poverty, but education is the key pathway toward empowerment. There is a lack of education for the children of present-day Latinos that underscore the culture and the achievements that are a part of its culture and our history. The majority of the education system during the primary and secondary years is underscored to teach a euro-education foundation.

The history of the United States, like the many of other countries, has as part of its rise and growth many instances of injustice. The Indian Removal Act signed into law by our 7th President Andrew Jackson began almost the indiscriminate policies of removing the Native Americans from their lands in the 1830s and resettling far North and West with as many as 25% dying as recorded in the Trail of Tears. During the revolutionary war the Indian tribes of the Cherokee, Chickasaw, Choctaw, Creek and Seminole Indians carried out important campaigns to help defeat the British. However, in a quest to rid of the Indians later to gain ownership of their land the use of Separation was used across the United States to Marginalize that culture. As with the Slave trade, the Chinese Exclusion Act, the Chinese Exclusion Act and the many laws that were discriminatory in nature against the Japanese. The mass exodus of the Irish to the United States during the Potato famine resulted in religious discrimination and led to the Bible Riots in 1844 in Philadelphia. The enslavement of blacks in the South who were considered property and the issues with the economics of slavery led to the Civil War. The discrimination that I felt growing up toward Latinos and those attitudes are still prevalent. It's the underbelly of the past and keeps our culture viewed as an underclass by many.

We will overcome it with time, education, demographics and as we become greater contributors economically. As a US Citizen that is part of our country's history, but Latinos ethnic heritage and culture will remain our foundation. We should not try to bury our past but accept that we will continue to get better, if we acknowledge it and keep it part of our past and not our future. By loosening the chains of ignorance through education and civility we can move forward even as it hurts. However, there is a significant achievement gap that exists and must be addressed aggressively within each family, community and the education system. The National Education Association (NEA) study indicates the percentage of Hispanics age 25 and older with a high school diploma or more was 52.4 percent in the 2000 census. This compared to 85.5 percent for Whites.

In addition, the percentage of Hispanics with bachelor's degrees or more was 10.4 percent, compared to 27 percent of Whites. From a competitive advantage position our young kids enter the job market playing catch-up. This is significant. Bilingual education has become pervasive as part of the education system, but it can be misleading. According to census data, approximately 80 of all English Language Learners (ELL) in the U.S are Hispanic. The majority of these students were born in the United States. Think about that. Nationwide, approximately 2.5 percent of teachers who instruct ELL possess a degree in ESL or bilingual education (NCES,1997. This disparity may account for the poor scores for ELL as reflected for English Language Arts which provide a measure of the critical thinking skills and writing. There continues to be increasing shortages for qualified candidates for jobs in science, technology, engineering and mathematics (STEM) and Latinos need to narrow the education gap as a whole and continue to be innovators. The Latino community needs to do more to ensure their children are equipped to be the top achievers in the education system. It is in the next 50 years that hopefully we will leave our legacy.

I grew up during beginnings of the Chicano movement and as Latinos we continue to contribute in meaningful ways to the United States. Latinos are the Future for U.S GDP Growth. From 2010 to 2017, the Latino GDP grew 28% faster than the rest of the U.S. economy, to $2.3 trillion in 2017. Since the financial crisis, Latinos have been responsible for 82% of the growth of the U.S Labor force, despite being only 18% of the overall population: (NJasinki,9/26/19, Barrons).

One day Latinos will no longer be a part of the minority in the United States and we need to be ready. The youth of today need to take the mantle.

Representing at Innovation forum

However, as we continue to become more an important part of our country here in the U.S. there will be others that will resist. I have met many people in all walks of life, young and old, those that are illiterate, and those who are PhDs, from Pittsburg to Europe and Asia and I have found that we have much in common. We all laugh, cry, and bleed. We as Chicanos, and as Americans, are not much different than each other even as we have our cultural differences. There are those that try to underscore the physical differences based on skin color or the class difference based on material wealth or education level, but these are only artificial in form. The history of our heritage and those others have many dimensions with struggles, prejudice, achievement mixed in. Each of us must continue to celebrate the uniqueness that our parents and ancestors have bestowed upon us as a gift and collectively we must all hope to endure with each other. We are scientists, mathematicians, astronauts, teachers, bankers, doctors, and are successfully part of many professions. We bring our salsa to the table and to the music and to our dance as we celebrate our rich history and the promise of our future.

As Latinos we must continue to keep our bar raised as we look to the future. Whatever type of career is chosen we must be respectful for the contribution that each one of us. Leadership programs are a must so that we can be influencers at the board level which Latinos are sorely lacking. But there are organizations that continue to recognize the contributions today and one is the California Latino Legislative Caucus with the annual Latino Spirit Awards, and there are others. Many of the honorees are pioneers in their respective fields and have overcome tremendous obstacles, rising to become role models and community leaders. (https://latinocaucus.legislature.ca.gov/latino-spirit-awards)

The percentage of Hispanics on Fortune 500 boards as of 2017 has been stagnant with only 2.7 percent having achieved those positions. More than 82 percent of Fortune 1000 companies still have no Hispanic Board members. We Chicanos must continue to educate the families and its youth on the Latino history and what impacts have been continually faced as part of racism and discrimination. These stories will underscore our resolve for the fight for equality and inclusion as we become a strong force in our country. Latinos must take the high ground and the Chicano movement must evolve from radicalism to education, to vote, and use the legal system to address and defeat laws that are discriminatory and racial at their core. The 50th anniversary of the Chicano Moratorium in Los Angeles approaches in 2020 and what remains to be seen is how we can all unite moving forward. It is time to re-tool for the future as legacy Chicanos transition the movement to the youth. We must not limit what we do to just Latinos we need to reach out to all those who are struggling as well and build bridges within ourselves and those who did not have the gift our heritage.

The Sureños and the Norteños will continue to be among us as part of the legacy of discrimination and racism and my hope is that they will eventually just be a small corner of our gente as our kids choose our familias and not the gangs. The Mexican American Political Association (MAPA) will continue to promote our interests as well as Hispanic and Mexican refugees in the United States, and Mexican American Legal and Education Fund (MALDEF) will continue to bring critical civil rights cases to the Supreme Court. But we must make the choices individually as we go forward with pride, education and passion.

This book is about my journey as a young child who has overcome the racism and discrimination of my time. I learned how to make choices for right and wrong, and enjoyed what others consider a career of success. But through it all I have always kept my culture and my heritage close and I could have not done any of it without my family. There is rage in the world, in our country and I have worked with so many who didn't understand our cultura. We have to take the high ground and embrace those that are different and educate those around us to reduce the level of ignorance. Let us not forget our history as we turn over the lessons to our children for the future. Let us live in the shadow of our parents and walk into the light of those of us who continue to succeed. We need to be proud, but always remember that our gente are humble as well.

We are descendants of the Mayans who were the earliest astronomers, mathematicians, developed the 365-year calendar to record the passages of time. We should acknowledge them as part of our lineage and go farther than we have. Some in my family were laborers and through their sacrifice their children were able to grow to their potential, understand what it is to be humble and be respectful as part of their lives. My oldest cousin Art worked as a director at Los Medanos College, my cousin Joseph worked in the far reaches of Alaska with Haliburton. My cousin Tom had children that went to Harvard, and my younger cousin Art was head of the design team for networking for Hewlett Packard and his son works in the Capital in Sacramento. My nephew attended UC Berkeley, his cousin went to Stanford, and my daughter graduated Summa Cum Laude from a college in New York. These children are the Latinos of the future, today. They are Americans proud of their family heritage and will go forward with positive aspirations and achievement.

When I was young I wanted to be an astronaut but that dream became a reality for other Latinos including; Jose Hernandez, Serena Auna, and Joseph Acaba. More and more Latinos are being elected in influential political offices including; Xavier Becerra as California Attorney General, with 38 members in Congress as of 2019 and including Sonia Sotomayor appointed by Barack Obama to the Supreme Court in 2009. Julian Castro, past HUD under Obama, has run for President. But this is not enough in today's world. We must continue to be a part of a transformational country and ensure through our heritage, our humanity, our education that we get a seat at the table to make positive change.

The challenge today in the 21st century is to continue to have an educated generation, ensure that we share our ideas, advocate the change of unjust laws and due process, and educate others with facts and push aside old beliefs. When I was young I heard the stories by our parents and grandparents and read the newspapers and watched TV to understand our world. Passion still exists when there is injustice and an example is the #Black Lives Matter movement, the #MeToo movement. Beyond protesting, change is needed and can be accelerated with new young women and men who we can vote for in elections. Social Media can be a powerful tool and serve as a catalyst for movements, just look at the 2019 Hong Kong protest demanding democratic reforms, change against police misconduct and other deep-rooted issues with over 2 million people participating in protests in June.

The recognition of fake news and how it shapes our perceptions should be taught in our schools. As an ethnic group Latinos can organize for positive change while at the same time respecting a wide range of views. Imagine if all the Puente, La Raza and Black Student Unions in the high schools and local community colleges could organize together for climate change, social justice, inclusion and empowerment. Then imagine if the issues presented linking and ideas for reform were extended to other community colleges in

California and beyond. It's all about the future. Moving forward the young will determine their fate and our future. All of us should try to continue to become active in their communities, understand the changes that are occurring and vote. Voting is a form of empowerment. We must provide testament to our humanity, and act with a voice and action for the new immigrants from Central America and other countries who look to us for hope. They seek asylum in our country, legally, due to oppression and likelihood of death for themselves and their family. We must remember that they left their families, their communities, and their countries for a chance for life. 95% will never see the southern borders or personally see or feel the despair by those who are stripped of hope. As of this publishing the Supreme Court has yet to rule on the fate of DACA (Deferred Action Children Arrivals) and whichever decision is made it will have a profound impact on over 640,000 registered Dreamers.

We are an imperfect nation with a history of overcoming our own internal prejudices to so many to this day. There is no perfect answer to the issues of the day, but we must challenge and debate our views to move forward.

I recall the poem by John Donne:
" Any man's death diminishes me, because I am involved in mankind; and therefore, never send to know for whom the bell tolls; it tolls for thee. "

The young must keep their bar raised. Latinos and non-Latinos alike. Education is the key to overcoming ignorance and making a lasting contribution. You can be more than you can imagine. Help others reach their goals as well. I am a futurist and I will be alive to see the Mission to Mars. Beyond that milestone I am hopeful for all the good that hopefully can overcome the negativity that we have to deal with daily.

As a technologist we will be on the next wave of innovation yet to be realized for example:
1. 3D manufacturing- clothes that respond to voice command to vary temperature
2. Retail Robots warehousing and delivery.
3. Artificial Intelligence for healthcare diagnostics via cell phones
4. Vertical food production using lasers and light-waves and reducing the need for water by 90% while producing what we need

But we must not forget our familias and our humanity as much as we move forward with technology. We can build walls, or we can build bridges to the future. There is much to be proud of and much to do. The present is made of the past, and the future is made of the present.

WHERE HAVE THE CHICANOS GONE

A REFLECTION: EDDIE SALAS

As the Years Go Passing By

Well there's nothing I can do
If you leave me here to cry (x2)
You know my love will follow you
As the years go passing by

I have long been a Santanista! It is ingrained into my Chicanismo, a feeling
and identity that I consciously embraced as a youth and daily, fight to
maintain as an adult. Yet, it is no longer viable in our Hispanic and Latino
world. And really, honestly "there is nothing I can do." It's the 21st century
and this edition of so-called Globalization has a wicked neo-liberal twist that
has captivated the minds and souls of a once proud and viable Chicano
nation. The old school self-determination and historical materialism has gone
awry with assimilationist patriotism and identity politics on steroids. I'm old,
I know. We are all older, we know, each of us in our own silence and not so
silent fight for our fleeting breaths, our dignity to remain standing. We are
now celebrating 27 years of el Cosmico Nopal Society de Aztlan c/s.

Where did the time go, where's so and so? Hey baby que paso, I
thought…. Arguments for and against time, the good, the bad and nimodo,
estan cabron and unfortunately all too real. Los once barrio boys made good
and retirado con papeles. We are los educados, the pioneers in many of our
familias who attended la U. And there are also those who didn't and remain
totally viable and stand amongst us con safos. From los fields and factories
to the office located across the spectrum of gainful employment. Que sura.
Made our jefitos proud, while allowing us to fulfill our hopes and dreams!
Not bad for campo, barrio, working class vatos. Not bad at all. El dilito es
that death and change are constants and if by chance we are standing, then
we surely pay homage to our muertos. De seguro. And it don't stop! Twenty
Seven. And counting. Orale! I miss my jefitos, I miss Favela, el Chief, Yeyo,
and Chicano Mike as I struggle to stay alive and remain productive and
Chicano. We all have our own caminos, our own vida locas, and our own
espinas. I just put mine out there but surely I have finally learned from my
jefito no less: "leave people the hell alone." So there is no judgment, no
ummm pues. Chale! One day at a time, como dice el Johnny. To each his
own, as the years go passing by.

Fact remains, not fake pero real. "As the Years Go Passing By" is a song penned by Peppermint Harris for Fenton Robinson, who first recorded it in 1959 for Duke Records, Duke #312. It is credited to be written by "Deadric Malone," a pseudonym for Don Robey, the owner of Duke Records. As the years went passing by Albert King (1967), Eric Burdon (1968), Carlos Santana (played it early in his career but not issued until 1997 – Live at the Fillmore 1968), The Elvin Bishop Group (1970), Al Kooper (1973), George Thorogood & the Destroyers (1982), Gary Moore (1990), Boz Scaggs (1990s), Booker T & the MGs (1990s), Otis Rush (1994) and the Jeff Henley Band (1995) each recorded their version. We know it best by Carlitos. The point being originality is truly a mix of a mezcla of our punto de vista at a specific time, which changes daily to become original then, only to change again with another's originality. In short, there ain't nothing new under the sun! La mizma gata nomas rebolcada. En Lak'ech, tu eres mi otro yo. Two sides of the same coin and on and on. It is the promise of the Fifth Sun in the Sixth and working on Seven Generations in the 27th year of el Nopal. We stand on the shoulders of those who came before us con safos. Los Grandes o sea los Chingones, como Joaquin reminds us.

I gave you all that I own
That's one thing you can't deny (x2)
You know my love will follow you
As the years go passing by

Where we at? Solos or collectively in the time of el Trompista, we DACA without Chicano Power yet we power the engine the ignites the protest that give los indocumentados their Amerikkkan Dream, as our Mesikan American lives get shattered into a million pedasos unless you educado and not addicted to drogas, sexo y la pobreza. In the time of "you have choices." We splintered between sun dances and alternative rock con pop cultura a la' Hip Hop, as hipsters rule the old new spaces of gentrification. And the economic downturn is up to lo mizmo capitalista exploits. As the years go passing by we get older and wiser and more illness than the young generations will ever know because the cure is a pill. Como dijo Alice, when she's ten feet tall. Chale! That too is old and played out. Maybe a fix, of radiation? We get caught off guard as we watch our elders parejas our loved ones fade into the sunset, setting us up to be the next in line? Como vez? Con mis ojos ese, only con stronger prescriptions. Maybe? Maybe we just roll with the punches cause Andres is still fighting Chevron in Richmond as sacred sites are out of sight and under new housing developments the second, third and fourth time around. Maybe? Maybe it just don't matter no more? No mo Mo, como decia Favela. Maybe self-determination and historical materialism was a Chicano Studies pair of dimes once upon a time? And now it's a watered down Ethnic Studies based on identity politics that rules, I mean rifa y controla ese. But

don't forget Mara and Cartel youth bring feria and jale to border patrols after mojarros.

At least we still gather! Los viejos espinosos. We hobble we wobble we show up we don't and won't for a million reasons but still we gather. A sacred circle dos tres chistes quemando unllas and David Martinez and su Margie stories con red red wine y la bud-weiser. We laugh and joke con abrazos and in silence we wonder quien sigue. It's not morbid it's life and we live it to the fullest, we would not gather we would not claim to be Nopaleros without the huevos to stand in the circle, okay sit pues. Still, aqui estamos y no nos vamos only con piernas cansados y sighs of relief to be sies pies arriba cause abajo we been many times before, so we gather canicosos and enjoy another breath another joke another joint session and corner conversations about our sacred lives in waning times poco pelo pero bien painado and trying hard not to lose our chile eating ability. Trying hard not to expose the trying times we live daily and at the same time for an Orale, just to be alive cause we are now old enough to truly understand los alternatives.

We have taken personal hits, all of us, la muerte sigue sigue sigue, la raza presente siempre but damn, will our pobre corazones ever find relief, una quebrada por favor. "That's just the way it is, some things will never change...." Creator have mercy on los de abajo turned professionals y que! Como siempre we are not exempt. Despite our tax exemptions we clearly live in the land of opportunity, which breeds los opportunists who chingar siempre. We can never escape the reality of our skin our personal histories upheld by that Primo Sister Tia y Abuelo who did not go to el post secondary education and reminds us painfully of where we come from. Where we have been before we have been to Disneyland and the cruse of a lifetime. Yes, we earned it. We paid for it! Just don't forget where we once walked where we once played tag and kissed for the first time in the neighborhoods of our youth where we left those who stayed behind for the millions of reasons that some don't gather this year. Remember a tree without roots, bears no fruit. 'Member tu pasado, tus suenos that help you stand in the space place you now call home.

I'm gonna leave it up to you
So long, so long good bye (x2)
You know my love will follow you
As the years go passing by

The Chinga, como decia Montoya is the fact that "community" in conjunto con los times de hoy are not what we ever imagined, never. It's a cruel hoax to believe that it's all good in the hood, as displacement of old stock home owners is called "progress." Politics have shift changed to accommodate a small number of folks con feria. Race matters as does class and we, la raza, is mo po than in all our lives. Yet our net worth is more cause we have mas gente, muchos in the minimum wages, immigrant y not. More youth que nunca, more grey como nosotros. Pero los lideres? Poli-tricks! Photo-ops y canela clashes and empty promises, except more police and less viable employment opportunities. Yes! We have made strides, huge ones but look behind us y no tanto. La U does not guarantee anything more than student loan debt. We are living witness to profound change and less consciousness less public talk less centro's y social service. Less less and less while we are more, mas y mas, more younger and still drop-out rates y baby's con babies remain amplio. Not so quiet shoot'em up bang bang gang bangers with no traditions who influence youth more than college recruiters. The Klickas influence more than ever y no one says nada cause our numbers grow unprecedented, daily, monthly, yearly. "Old folks say there's no hope for the youth, truth is there's no hope for the future," said Tupac. He dead too. And His n Her panic Republicans say there is no climate change. Yet, it's getting hotter out here.

Nom'bre we are living witness to profound change at the local level. Global local cambio social and younger acacademicos have no concept of where we been! Where we going tampoco. No mo critical dialogue in the faces of Homeland security as co-intel-pro has a new face that looks like ours y lo de mas color folk. We have lived through much! We continue to live through much mucho much more than we ever could have imagined con technology that is out of this world, literally. It's like a jungle sometimes, it makes me wonder how we keep from going under? We are Nopaleros in the age of the "I." Older vatos standing in the face of adversity con memories of a time gone by, as even the musica has changed on us. Damn we old(errr)! One last thought (yeah right), this year can we agree to bring some comida saludable. Like more fruits n veggies! Cause as the years go passing by our health matters most and there will be a next year, believe that, with or without us. Nos vemos espinosos. Que se cuiden cabrones!

Escito por el Salas Con Safos en el ano de fake news y el polyester prez Dos Mil Diez y siete
Que reine la Paz, Mamacita have mercy on us!

INSPIRATION

I have written this journey for my daughter. I hope that she will understand our Raza and me better with the words that I have shared. Mija, I have been inspired by so many in my lifetime but as I reflect upon my greatest inspiration, it is you, my daughter. You are the one who provided the fulfillment that was missing for so many years, and as I watched you grow up I could quickly see that you were all that I was not. The drive to succeed, the compassion for others, and joy for life was part of your every-day life. I will always remember the joy I felt when as you were first born your eyes locked with mine as part of your new life. You are my only child and even as I traveled far and wide in my career you I worked to pour the best of me to be part of you. I keep in my heart that sunny day at your Nanny and Papas house in Derby, New York when you were about 9 months old. You were in your stroller and you looked up high through the tree the first time that you heard the voice and the song of the young bird starting its own life. I will never forget it. I remember when we were living in New York and I had come inside of our house after working to take care of our huge backyard in the fall. You asked me for a couple of cupcakes that I had brought home for you the night before. You put 2 candles in them, and you took outside and as your Mom turned around to see what was going on, you sat down on the grass and said; "Mom, let's have a picnic."

We had our Daddy days and they were joyful, and you were always so curious about everything around you. When you needed me, you would say to me "Help You, Help You" and I always was there for you. I was awed by how you learned to play the piano, starting at 3 years old, then the flute, then you taught yourself the other instruments as well. I listened to you sing every day it seemed in your young life and the feeling of pride as you sang at Carnegie Hall and Lincoln Center in New York with your school. You were always competitive, and I saw that fire as you played Libero for your Volleyball teams and captained your bowling teams. I remember one day coming home early, quietly walking into the house, and you were singing in Italian for an Honors Competition in Buffalo.

I remember the time that you were playing softball when you were 8 years old, and you were pitching, and the hitter hit the ball toward you. I saw you take a step and suddenly stop. I watched the young girl at third base finally grab the ball and tossed it to first base. You told me later, as you showed me your compassion, that you could have made the play, but you wanted the 3rd baseman to feel what it was like to make the play. I gave you more hugs than you can ever remember, trust me. In Buffalo I took you with me to work as part of Father/Daughter day and I remember you asking me which button you could push as I took you into the computer room. You had your challenges in your life, but you overcame them and always had a smile and had so many positive friends around you. I remember how you immersed yourself working with people as part of the triple A team of the New York Mets and the NHL Buffalo Sabres in Guest Services in the HSBC Arena.

I was able to be witness and be a part of your joys as you grew up. As you grew into a young woman I always asked that "Be yourself, believe in yourself, and always do your best", and you always did. I have always marveled by how you took this life you were given and continue to help others as you go through your own journey.

Summa Cum Laude!!!

You come from a rich heritage and hopefully you can understand your dad a little bit better. Continue to go forth and embrace all that life has to offer.

You will be forever young in my heart.

SHOUT OUT

I would be remiss if I did not give a shout-out to so many of my friends those who continue to inspire me to get off the couch and work with others for peace and humanity.

Cosmico Nopal Society de Aztlan: To my many brothers who I respect and have shared our spirits together as we recognize that we are only a shadow of the greatness of our parents, grandparents and familia.

Eddie Salas: I have known for over 45 years and with whom we have shared our collective experiences and how we embrace what we have and what we want to impart to our youth. Eddie's relentless passion on supporting mental health to give young kids hope has made a tremendous difference.

Johnny Rodriguez: Has made a difference to families and the youth, those who were at-risk, and those who he has imparted the qualities of positive action. As Executive Director of One Day at a Time (ODAT) for over 20 years his leadership and passion for helping the community cannot be measured, but only felt. Honored as Citizen of the Year in Brentwood and elected to City Council shows how the community feels about his work.

Heliodoro Moreno: He walks the walk. From the abyss of his youth, to serving in Iraq and Afghanistan, to education through law school and providing help to immigrants he is a model of the young Chicano. He continues to give back to his community and inspire the youth as President of Future Leaders of America.

Danny Lopez; An immigrant from Mexico, working to create his own Web Branding Company, founder of Gateway Rotary, his spirit of community and reaching out to different groups has showed the way. His and organizing efforts with others for inspired events has made Pittsburg an inclusive community.

Mary Rocha: Contra Costa woman of the year. As non-profit founder, as school board member, as Mayor of Antioch her relentless pursuit of making change has made her a treasure for us all. Her legacy in Antioch for helping those who need it most will always is indomitable.

David Littleton: The ultimate educator. Balu, since the first time I came under your tutelage in high school you have continued to teach me about the truth and to challenge the injustices that surround us.

Gregory Osorio: A humble man with great spirit and founder of non-profits for social justice, he has mentored our youth and helped them lead. The Martin Luther King Tribute, the Cesar Chavez/Dolores Huerta March and Tribute and others are all possible because of Gregory.

Paul Ramirez: The embodiment of the true Chicano. He continues to do the work that needs to be done. The Chairman of the East Bay United Latino

Voices he was instrument in driving the change for DACA in Contra Costa County, leads the effort to ensure success for the annual Cesar Chavez Awards and holds those in office accountable. His pursuit of justice is driven with educating others, facilitating discussions, and driving positive action.

Mr. Cornelius; My Science teacher in Central Junior high who instilled in me the search for the unknown and helped me to understand how to research and go beyond what was taught in class.

Mr. Arenivar; You are timeless and ageless. Your athletic feats as an athlete were recognized and finally they named the high school baseball field for you. Your leadership on the Pittsburg School Board throughout the years shows how much you care about our community and our kids.

Mr. Chacon, Mr. Massey, Mr. Gloria, Mr. Gilliam, Mr. Caldwell, Coach Galli, and Mr. Sullenberger, you were the teachers, and advisors, who I needed as I grew up and I thank you all.

Dolores Huerta: As the Co-Founder of the United Farmworkers Union she continues to rally and help the poor, senior citizens, and those who need a voice for their civil rights to make the future better. So, Dolores, thank you so much for your spirit and the words that you shouted long ago, that I will never forget:

Si Se Puede

NOTES
PICTURES AND REFERENCES

Mom: The Big T

My Father -Jesus Sandoval

My beloved Tia Chelo and my Tio Joe. I can still hear his laughter.

My Home boys. Chief, Me, Yeyo, Jerry and my cousin George

Street Life: Boys From the Burg

Sister Grace, Eleuterio, and Yeyo. Yeyo bro, you were the man.

My Mom, her granddaughter Monique (Irene's daughter) and sister Erma

1)Silent Spring: https://en.wikipedia.org/wiki/Silent_Spring

Silent Spring is an environmental science book by Rachel Carson. The book was published on September 27, 1962, documenting the adverse environmental effects caused by the indiscriminate use of pesticides. Carson accused the chemical industry of spreading disinformation, and public officials of accepting the industry's marketing claims unquestioningly. It spurred a reversal in the United States' national pesticide policy, led to a nationwide ban on DDT for agricultural uses, and helped to inspire an environmental movement that led to the creation of the U.S. Environmental Protection Agency

2)USS Enterprise: https://en.wikipedia.org/wiki/USS_Enterprise_(CVN-65)

USS Enterprise (CVN-65), formerly CVA(N)-65, is a decommissioned [14] United States Navy aircraft carrier. She was the first nuclear-powered aircraft carrier and the eighth United States naval vessel to bear the name. Like her predecessor of World War II fame, she is nicknamed "Big E". At 1,123 feet (342 m),[6][7] she is the longest naval vessel ever built. Her 93,284-long-ton (94,781 t)[5] displacement ranks her as the 12th-heaviest carrier, after the ten carriers of the Nimitz class and USS Gerald R. Ford. Enterprise had a crew of some 4,600 service members

3) The Global Financial Crisis of 2008: https://en.wikipedia.org/wiki/Financial_crisis_of_2007–2008

The financial crisis of 2007–2008, also known as the global financial crisis and the 2008 financial crisis, is considered by many economists to have been the most serious financial crisis since the Great Depression of the 1930s.

It began in 2007 with a crisis in the subprime mortgage market in the United States. It developed into a full-blown international banking crisis with the collapse of the investment bank Lehman Brothers on September 15, 2008. Excessive risk-taking by banks such as Lehman Brothers helped to magnify the financial impact globally. Massive bail-outs of financial institutions and other palliative monetary and fiscal policies were employed to prevent a possible collapse of the world financial system. The crisis was nonetheless followed by a global economic downturn, the Great Recession.

4)QRM-Quantitative_Risk_Management :
https://www.qrm.com/Whatwedo/Assetliabilitymanagementmarketrisk/assetliabilitymanage
mentmarketrisk.htm

In the Asset-Liability & Market Risk engagement, client's partner with QRM consultants and Subject Matter Experts who have years of experience modeling, measuring, and managing risk.

5) AssetLiabilityManagement:

ALM is the process of evaluating and executing actions to control the bank's risks and reach its financial goals. The role of ALM has a very broad reach and goes beyond just Interest Rate Risk Management. Notice there are several key words or phrases in the above definition of ALM. First, ALM is a process. You can have the best ALM model and the people to run it, however if the process is incorrect, you may be missing opportunities within the bank. As mentioned earlier, at a minimum, it must be coordinated with the Long-Range Planning Process and the Budgeting Process. Since people and systems make a process work effectively, all parties involved must work together to coordinate these disciplines.

6)   Pentagon Papers:

The Pentagon Papers was the name given to a top-secret Department of Defense study of U.S. political and military involvement in Vietnam from 1945 to 1967. As the Vietnam War dragged on, with more than 500,000 U.S. troops in Vietnam by 1968, military analyst Daniel Ellsberg—who had worked on the study—came to oppose the war and decided that the information contained in the Pentagon Papers should be available to the American public.

7)   NavalBaseSubicBay:

Naval Base Subic Bay was a major ship-repair, supply, and rest and recreation facility of the Spanish Navy and subsequently the United States Navy located in Zambales, Philippines. The base was 262 square miles, about the size of Singapore. The Vietnam War was the period of peak activity as Subic Bay became the U.S. Seventh Fleet forward base for repair and replenishment after the Gulf of Tonkin incident in 1964. The average number of ships visiting the base per month rose from 98 in 1964 to 215 by 1967.

8)   SubprimeMortgageCrisis:

The United States subprime mortgage crisis was a nationwide financial crisis, occurring between 2007 and 2010, that contributed to the U.S. recession of December 2007 – June 2009.[1][2] It was triggered by a large decline in home prices after the collapse of a housing bubble, leading to mortgage delinquencies and foreclosures and the devaluation of housing-related securities. While elements of the crisis first became more visible during 2007, several major financial institutions collapsed in September 2008, with significant disruption in the flow of credit to businesses and consumers and the onset of a severe global recession

9) Salaices : http://www.salaices.com/history.htm

The history of the Salaices family. After the Aztec empire fell, the legend about a fabulously rich place began to circulate among the Spaniards. The legend centered on various places in the north, including La Florida, Las Siete Ciudades de Cíbola, Nuevo México, Quivira, Marata, and Cópala. The discovery of mines in Santa Bárbara (Santa Bárbola), in what is now the state of Chihuahua, inspired some of the expeditions that were looking for the legendary place. The Spaniards continued to arrive during a long period that began with the first expeditions by conquistadors until the War of Independence. Based on the statistics, it appears that the immigrant boom occurred toward end of the 1600s and the beginning of the 1700s. Many families moved directly from Spain to the southern region of Nueva Vizcaya (New Spain's northern territories). Spanish immigrants to reach Nueva Vizcaya included miners, farmers, and livestock ranchers; also, soldiers, tradesmen, government civil servants, and others. The Salaices arrived at some point during these migrations.

10) Tuna Canneries: https://sandiegohistory.org/journal/v58-1/v58-1felando.pdf

Canning of tuna, however, did not become an industry in the United States until 1903. Because of the uncertainty of the sardine supply as a result of the sardine shortage of 1902, Southern California fishermen searched for new types of fish to can. Albert P. Halfhill, cofounder of the San Pedro-based canning firm, the California Fish Company, was one of the first developers of tuna canning in California. Although Halfhill's canned albacore was unpopular at first in the Los Angeles area, his shipments to New York were successful enough to create an "instantaneous" demand.

11) SanDiego Canneries: https://www.chicanoparkmuseum.org/logan-heights-archival-project/logan-heights-canneries/

The demand for albacore in the East Coast caused the tuna industry to boom and fostered the rapid construction of canneries along the coast of Southern California. From the years of 1911- 1912, five new canneries opened in the ports of San Pedro, Wilmington, Long Beach, and San Diego. San Diego's first tuna cannery was called the Pacific Tuna Canning Company and it was located in what is known today as Logan Heights. The community during the height of the industry, the early 1950s, was one that was very diverse and one that generated approximately $65 million for its 17,000 locals.

12) History-Forgotten-Japantown: http://www.californiajapantowns.org/Isleton.pdf

Similar to other Delta towns, Isleton grew with the rich peat soil from the river, ideal for agriculture and prides itself as the "Asparagus Capital of the

World". In 1919, Thomas Foon Chew founded Bayside Cannery at Isleton and brought his processing experience to the Delta, becoming the first to package green asparagus. In the early 1900s, the Japanese laborers followed the path to the Delta. Through hardwork and dexterity, the Japanese comprised 31.7% of the agricultural labor force in the region by 1910, nearing the 41.5% whites and exceeding the 24.9% Chinese. At its peak,

Isleton had five canneries, including industry leaders, H.J. Heinz Company and Libby, McNeil, and Libby.

13) Historic Locke: https://www.nps.gov/places/locke-historic-district.htm

The Locke Historic District, also known as the town of Locke, California, was built in 1915 by Chinese immigrants from Heungshan [Xiangshan] County (modern day Zhongshan), in Guangdong Province, China. When the railroad was completed in 1869, thousands of Chinese laborers, primarily from Guangdong Province, were hired to work on an extensive levee project in California's Sacramento-San Joaquin River Delta. Their knowledge of how to develop farmland in river valleys, learned from farming the Pearl River Delta region in southern China, was used to construct a large network of earthen levees that eventually turned 500,000 acres of swamp into some of California's most valuable farmland. The town of Locke was founded in 1915, after a fire destroyed the Chinese community in Walnut Grove. Locke was the last of the Sacramento River Chinatowns to be built and became a thriving Chinese community serving the area's workforce, which consisted mainly of Chinese laborers working in the asparagus fields.

14) Early Pittsburg History- 1917 – Per Otis Loveridge : http://history.rays-place.com/ca/cc-pittsburg.htm

A townsite was surveyed and christened "New York of the Pacific." Upon the discovery of coal near Mount Diablo, about fifty years ago, the place became known as Black Diamond. It is believed that a large coal field in that region still remains undeveloped. In 1909 the present name of Pittsburg was appropriately bestowed; the town having shown conclusively that it was to become a great manufacturing center.

15) Isola de Femme to Pittsburg: https://giamona.com/news.html

Since the 1870s, California's Italian immigrant fishermen and their sons and grandsons have stalked salmon, sardines, squid, snapper, sole, sharks, sand dabs and dozens of other sea creatures with unrivaled skill and passion from Peru to the Bering Sea. They launched fleets from Monterey to Eureka, revolutionized fishing techniques with their lampara ("lightning") nets, and quickly developed California into the second-largest fishery in the nation. Their children included former San Francisco Mayor Joe Alioto and baseball legend Joe DiMaggio. And they enchanted writers such as Jack London, who drank with them in Pittsburg, and John Steinbeck, who sailed with them from Cannery Row to the Sea of Cortez. Italians had been fishing the Sacramento River since the Gold Rush, and the first fish cannery on the West Coast opened in Sacramento in 1864. By the turn of the century, Ferrante and other immigrants had turned Pittsburg -- then called Black Diamond --into an Italian fishing village of 2,000.

16) Ferdinand Marcos: https://www.thoughtco.com/ferdinand-marcos-195676
Ferdinand Marcos (Sept. 11, 1917–Sept. 28, 1989) ruled the Philippines with an iron fist from 1966 to 1986. Critics charged Marcos and his regime with crimes like corruption and nepotism. Marcos himself is said to have exaggerated his role in World War II. He also murdered a family political rival. Marcos created an elaborate cult of personality. When that state-mandated adulation proved insufficient for him to maintain control, President Marcos declared martial law.

17) Vietnam Peace Accords: https://learning.blogs.nytimes.com/2012/01/23/jan-23-1973-nixon-announces-end-of-u-s-involvement-in-vietnam/

18) Operation-FrequentWind   :
https://en.wikipedia.org/wiki/Operation_Frequent_Wind
Operation Frequent Wind was the final phase in the evacuation of American civilians and "at-risk" Vietnamese from Saigon, South Vietnam prior to the takeover of the city by the North Vietnamese People's Army of Vietnam (PAVN) in the Fall of Saigon.

19) I am Joaquin: https://en.wikipedia.org/wiki/I_Am_Joaquin
I Am Joaquin (also known as Yo soy Joaquin), by Rodolfo "Corky" Gonzales, is a famous epic poem associated with the Chicano movement of the 1960s in the United States. In I am Joaquin, Joaquin (the narrative voice of the poem) speaks of the struggles that the Chicano people have faced in trying to achieve economic justice and equal rights in the U.S, as well as to find an identity of being part of a hybrid mestizo society.

20) CesarChavez/DoloresHuerta-UnitedFarmWorkersUnion
https://en.wikipedia.org/wiki/Cesar_Chavez
Cesar Chavez (born César Estrada Chávez, locally [ˈsesaɾ esˈtɾaða ˈtʃaβes]; March 31, 1927 – April 23, 1993) was an American labor leader and Latino American civil rights activist. Along with Dolores Huerta, he co-founded the National Farm Workers Association, later renamed the United Farm Workers (UFW) union. His public-relations approach to unionism and aggressive but nonviolent tactics made the farm workers' struggle a moral cause with nationwide support. By the late 1970s, his tactics had forced

growers to recognize the UFW as the bargaining agent for 50,000 field workers in California and Florida.

21) The Brutal History of Anti-Latino Discrimination in America- Erin Blakemore:

https://www.history.com/news/the-brutal-history-of-anti-latino-discrimination-in-america

The story of Latino-American discrimination largely begins in 1848, when the United States won the Mexican-American War. The Treaty of Guadalupe Hidalgo, which marked the war's end, granted 55 percent of Mexican territory to the United States. With that land came new citizens. The Mexicans who decided to stay in what was now U.S. territory were granted citizenship and the country gained a considerable Mexican American population.

As the 19th century wore on, political events in Mexico made emigration to the United States popular. This was welcome news to American employers like the Southern Pacific Railroad, which desperately needed cheap labor to help build new tracks. The railroad and other companies flouted existing immigration laws that banned importing contracted labor and sent recruiters into Mexico to convince Mexicans to emigrate

22) Immigration Act of 1924- Julia Young

https://blogs.loc.gov/kluge/2015/03/the-history-of-mexican-immigration-to-the-u-s-in-the-early-20th-century/

The flow of immigrants from Mexico into the United States during the 19th and early 20th centuries.

For almost a half-century after the annexation of Texas in 1845, the flow was barely a trickle. In fact, there was a significant migration in the other direction: Mexican citizens who left the newly annexed U.S. territories and resettled in Mexican territory.

Beginning around the 1890s, new industries in the U.S. Southwest-especially mining and agriculture-attracted Mexican migrant laborers. The Mexican Revolution (1910-1920) then increased the flow: war refugees and political exiles fled to the United States to escape the violence. Mexicans also left rural areas in search of stability and employment. As a result, Mexican migration to the United States rose sharply. The number of legal migrants grew from around 20,000 migrants per year during the 1910s to about 50,000 – 100,000 migrants per year during the 1920. Mexico was exempted from the quotas in the Immigration Act of 1924.

Mexico (and in fact, the entire Western hemisphere) was exempt from the quotas in part because of the agricultural lobby: farmers in the U.S. Southwest argued that without Mexican migrants, they would be unable to find the laborers needed to sow and harvest their crops. In addition, migration from the Western Hemisphere made up less than one-third of the overall flow of migrants to the United States at the time. Finally, the perceptions of Mexicans as temporary migrants and docile laborers contributed to the fact that they were never included in the quotas.

23) The Deadly Pixley Cotton Strike and Impacts: https://www.thegoodlifesv.com/story/2016/09/01/history/the-deadly-pixley-cotton-strike/271.html

As the amount of irrigated land in California increased in the early 1900s, so did the need for farm workers. The workers came, and unionization soon followed. Job actions became common and between 1933-1939 California had 180 strikes involving nearly 90,000 workers. One of the strikes occurred in Tulare County, and in 1933 the little town of Pixley became ground zero for a bloody incident. The farmworkers had left the fields and were demonstrating against the low wages while the cotton rotted unpicked. What followed next was the murder of some of crowd by local growers and after the trial these men were set free.

24) Mexican Revolution: https://en.wikipedia.org/wiki/Mexican_Revolution

The Mexican Revolution (Spanish: Revolución mexicana), also known as the Mexican Civil War (Spanish: guerra civil mexicana), was a major armed struggle, lasting roughly from 1910 to 1920, that transformed Mexican cultureand government. This armed conflict is often characterized as the most important sociopolitical event in Mexico and one of the greatest upheavals of the 20th century.

25) Erwin Rommel-Desert Fox: https://en.wikipedia.org/wiki/Erwin_Rommel

Johannes Erwin Eugen Rommel (15 November 1891 – 14 October 1944) was a German general and military theorist. Popularly known as the Desert Fox, he served as field marshal in the Wehrmacht (Defense Force) of Nazi Germany during World War II, as well as serving in the Reichswehr of the Weimar Republic, and the army of Imperial Germany.

26) Chicano Moratorium: https://en.wikipedia.org/wiki/Chicano_Moratorium

The Chicano Moratorium, formally known as the National Chicano Moratorium Committee, was a movement of Chicano anti-war activists that built a broad-based coalition of Mexican-American groups to organize opposition to the Vietnam War. Led by activists from local colleges and members of the "Brown Berets", a group with roots in the high school student movement that staged walkouts in 1968, the coalition peaked with an August 29, 1970 march in East Los Angeles that drew 30,000 demonstrators.

27) Chicanismo: https://en.wikipedia.org/wiki/Chicanismo

Chicanismo is the ideology behind the Chicano movement. It is an ideology based on a number of important factors that helped shape a social uprising in order to fight for the liberties of Mexican Americans. Chicanismo was shaped by a number of intellectuals and influential activists as well as by the artistic and political sphere, and the many contributors to the ideology collaborated to create a strong sense of self-identity within the Chicano community.

28) Father of Supercomputing: https://en.wikipedia.org/wiki/Seymour_Cray

Seymour Roger Cray (September 28, 1925[1] – October 5, 1996[2]) was an American electrical engineer and supercomputer architect who designed a series of computers that were the fastest in the world for decades, and founded Cray Research which built many of these machines. Called "the father of supercomputing",[2] Cray has been credited with creating the supercomputer industry. Joel S. Birnbaum, then chief technology officer of Hewlett-Packard, said of him: "It seems impossible to exaggerate the effect he had on the industry; many of the things that high performance computers now do routinely were at the farthest edge of credibility when Seymour envisioned them. Larry Smarr, then director of the National Center for Supercomputing Applications at the University of Illinois said that Cray is "the Thomas Edison of the supercomputing industry.

https://www.computerhistory.org/revolution/supercomputers/10/22

"One of my guiding principles" observed Seymour Cray, "is, 'don't do anything that other people are Doing."

Cray was a brilliant, soft-spoken computer designer who made a career of building the world's fastest computers, time and again. He preferred working in small teams, undisturbed by managers. Or better still, working alone at night, free from interruptions.

Cray's quirky work habits were matched by his unusual diversions, which included digging tunnels under his house and, once, burning a boat he had built because he'd built a new one.

29) Howard Hughes: https://en.wikipedia.org/wiki/Howard_Hughes

Howard Robard Hughes Jr. (December 24, 1905 – April 5, 1976) was an American business magnate, investor, record-setting pilot, engineer,[4] film director, and philanthropist, known during his lifetime as one of the most financially successful individuals in the world. He first became prominent as a film producer, and then as an influential figure in the aviation industry. Later in life, he became known for his eccentric behavior and reclusive lifestyle—oddities that were caused in part by a worsening obsessive–compulsive disorder (OCD), chronic pain from a near-fatal plane crash and increasing deafness.

Hughes formed the Hughes Aircraft Company in 1932, hiring numerous engineers and designers. He spent the rest of the 1930s and much of the 1940s setting multiple world air speed records and building the Hughes H-1 Racer and H-4 Hercules (the Spruce Goose). He acquired and expanded

Trans World Airlines and later acquired Air West, renaming it Hughes Airwest. Hughes was included in Flying Magazine's list of the 51 Heroes of Aviation, ranked at No. 25.[7] Today, his legacy is maintained through the Howard Hughes Medical Institute and the Howard Hughes Corporation

30) George Boole: https://en.wikipedia.org/wiki/Boolean_algebra

Boolean algebra was introduced by George Boole in his first book The Mathematical Analysis of Logic (1847), and set forth more fully in his An Investigation of the Laws of Thought (1854). Boolean algebra has been fundamental in the development of digital electronics, and is provided for in all modern programming languages. It is also used in set theory and statistics.

31) Edward Teller: https://en.wikipedia.org/wiki/Edward_Teller

Edward Teller (Hungarian: Teller Ede; January 15, 1908 – September 9, 2003) was a Hungarian-American theoretical physicist who is known colloquially as "the father of the hydrogen bomb" (see the Teller–Ulam design), although he did not care for the title.[1] He made numerous contributions to nuclear and molecular physics, spectroscopy (in particular the Jahn–Teller and Renner–Teller effects), and surface physics..[3] Throughout his life, Teller was known both for his scientific ability and for his difficult interpersonal relations and volatile personality.

32) Mass Deportations: https://www.history.com/news/great-depression-repatriation-drives-mexico-deportation

In the 1930s, the Los Angeles Welfare Department decided to start deporting hospital patients of Mexican descent. The logic behind these raids was that Mexican immigrants were supposedly using resources and working jobs that should go to white Americans affected by the Great Depression.

33) Latino Spirit Awards:. https://latinocaucus.legislature.ca.gov/latino-spirit-awards

The Latino Spirit Awards were established in 2002 at the State Capitol in Sacramento to coincide with our states acknowledgement of Cinco de Mayo and highlight positive role models in our community. Every year, the Caucus honors Latinos/as in a variety of categories that range from athletics/sports, to public service and human right.

ABOUT THE AUTHOR

FERNANDO SANDOVAL

Chicano Activist with background in Information Technology and a Business consultant for International Banking.

Born in Sacramento with family heritage from Mexico and initially raised in a Cannery Labor Camp. Raised by a single mother of 4 became an early activist supporting the Boycotts of the late 60s, member of the Brown Berets and member of Teatro Carlitos. Served in Vietnam and Thailand. Global Relationship Manager, HSBC Bank. International Banking Consultant for Capital Markets based in Belgium. Attended the University of Connecticut/State University of New York

Contributor to the following:

United Latino Voices of Contra Costa County
Hispanic Chamber of Contra Costa County
Pittsburg Unified School District
Citizens Bond Oversight Committee
Contra Costa Taxpayers Association,
Cesar Chavez/Dolores Huerta Tribute Planning Committee,
Rotary- New York: Past President; Gateway Rotary- Vice President
District Equal Employment Advisory Opportunity Council
Community College District

Books to provide insights- Just a few

Youth Identity and Power- Carlos Muniz

The Promise of the Fifth Sun- Dr. Jorge Partida

Becoming Mexican American- George J Sanchez

Over the Edge of the World- Laurence Bergreen

Aztec- Gary Jennings

Counselor- Ted Sorensen

Caveat: Reagan, Realism and Foreign Affairs – Gen Alexander Haig

No More Vietnams- Richard Nixon

Made in the USA
Columbia, SC
18 February 2020